PORTPATRICK TO DONAGHADEE

THE ORIGINAL SHORT SEA ROUTE

BY

FRASER G. MacHAFFIE

Published by

STRANRAER AND DISTRICT LOCAL HISTORY TRUST

ISBN   0 9535776-7-8

© 2001 Fraser G. MacHaffie

Published by
Stranraer and District Local History Trust
Tall Trees
London Road
Stranraer DG9 8BZ

PORTPATRICK to DONAGHADEE:
THE ORIGINAL SHORT SEA ROUTE

FRASER G. MacHAFFIE

Contents

Introduction

ONE MILE OUT OF PORTPATRICK, a milestone tells us we are 7 miles from Stranraer, 83 miles from Dumfries and 415 miles from London. We understand Stranraer and, possibly, Dumfries, but London? The milestone dates from 1808 and a map of a few years before shows the principal roads in Ireland. A road is shown running from Dublin to Donaghadee in County Down, but not to Belfast. Why were the connections between Dublin and Donaghadee so important? This booklet attempts to explain.

Saint Patrick, so legend has it, crossed in one stride from Scotland to Ireland. Sceptics were directed to the footprint left on a rock at the port bearing his name. On another occasion, Patrick swam across to Ireland from the port, holding his severed head in his teeth (surely only the Apostle of Ireland could achieve that feat!). In this publication I hope to give an account of the route developed by lesser mortals between Portpatrick and Donaghadee, a route which could as well be associated with Saint Jude, the patron saint of lost causes, as with Saint Patrick.

By the middle of the seventeenth century, the name Portpatrick was in use reflecting the long-established traffic through the port of pilgrimages to Saul, County Down, with the purpose of visiting the grave of Patrick. The pilgrims availed themselves of both the shelter provided by the Chapel Patrick in the village and the small harbours laid down by nature at both Portpatrick and Donaghadee.

In the opening years of the seventeenth century, there had been a significant move of Scottish settlers into northern Down and Antrim in Ulster. This migration was with the encouragement of the crown and land was given to these settlers and "plantations" were established. Family and commercial ties added to the traffic between Scotland and Ireland and the short route between Portpatrick and Donaghadee was the route of choice. By 1605, Hugh Montgomerie had obtained land in Down and fifteen years later he purchased land around Portpatrick. It is from this period on that reliable records rather than legends have survived and so we take up the story. Extracts from contemporary accounts are used where they add to our understanding of the times.

Much of the material of this publication has appeared previously in the first five chapters of The Short Sea Route, published in 1975 and long out of print.

Fraser G. MacHaffie
Marietta College
Marietta, Ohio
June, 2001

A BRIEF CHRONOLOGY

1616 Hugh Montgomerie receives ferry rights for Donaghadee-Portpatrick.

1626 Harbour at Donaghadee completed.

1770 John Smeaton begins construction of harbour at Portpatrick.

1774 John Smeaton completes work at Portpatrick Harbour.

July 1791 Contract signed between Post Office and Donaghadee Packet Company for daily mail service.

1820 Work begins on John Rennie's plans for Portpatrick Harbour.

1821 Work begins on John Rennie's plans for Donaghadee Harbour.

4 May 1825 Steampackets *Dasher* and *Arrow* start Post Office service.

January 1837 Responsibility for mail packet service transferred to Admiralty.

February 1838 Work on rebuilding of Donaghadee Harbour completed.

September 1847 Harbour Commissioners at Portpatrick hand over responsibility for harbour to Admiralty.

July 1849 Mail route between Scotland and Ireland transferred to Greenock-Belfast.

15 August 1856 Treasury Minute supporting Portpatrick-Donaghadee route.

May 1858 Construction of Portpatrick Railway started.

11 March 1861 Railway opened linking Stranraer and Castle-Douglas (and Dumfries).

3 June 1861 Railway opened linking Donaghadee and Newtownards (and Belfast).

28 August 1862 Railway opened linking Portpatrick and Stranraer (and Castle-Douglas).

January 1863 Admiralty hand over responsibility for Portpatrick Harbour to the Board of Trade.

24 July 1863 Water admitted to North Basin at Portpatrick.

1866 Work at Portpatrick Harbour ceases.

13 July 1868 Donaghadee & Portpatrick Short Sea Steam Packet Company, Ltd. begins twice-daily (except Sunday) service with paddle steamer *Dolphin*. Lasted until October 1868.

1870 *Reliance* on summer service between Donaghadee and Portpatrick.

1871 *Aber* on summer service between Donaghadee and Portpatrick.

1873 *Avalon* on summer service between Donaghadee and Portpatrick.

1874 Rails of harbour branch at Portpatrick lifted.

1891 *Terrible* on summer service between Donaghadee and Portpatrick.

6 February 1950 Railway linking Portpatrick and Stranraer closed.

April 1950 Railway linking Donaghadee and Belfast closed.

1. THE DAY BEFORE YESTERDAY

As the seventeenth century opened, Ireland was enjoying a period of unusual peace. During the decades of rest from strife, the Tudor policy of settling "plantations" in Ireland continued (Elizabeth I had discovered that it was easier and cheaper to "civilise" the Irish by moving in loyal and land-hungry subjects than treat much of the east coast of the island as a military garrison). A centralised government was established in Dublin. The policy gained momentum under the Stuart monarchs, starting with James VI and I in 1603. The plantations created a demand for reliable routes for trade and communication between Britain and Ireland. In particular, Down and Antrim had been settled by adventurers from Scotland and the 21-mile sea crossing between Portpatrick in Galloway and Donaghadee in County Down took on a new importance.

The earliest surviving written document relevant to the Portpatrick-Donaghadee route is dated 15th January 1616. The document indicates a route already in frequent use and is concerned with regulating traffic by preventing the "dailie disorders in conveyinge of stolen goodes" and the "bringinge in of idle and lewd people to the huindrance of the Plantacion." The document was in response to concern raised in April 1615 at the Scottish Privy Council in Edinburgh over unchecked travel and movement of goods between Scotland and Ireland (The Privy Council was, in effect, "running" Scotland after the departure of James VI to London on becoming James I of England). The document, completed at Dublin Castle, the seat of Irish administration, is addressed to the Attorney General in London and requests the awarding of letters patent (i.e. exclusive rights) to Sir Hugh Montgomerie whereby Donaghadee would be the only port along that part of the coast where passengers and goods could be landed or leave. Further, Montgomerie was to be given the ferry rights between Donaghadee and Portpatrick and begin construction of a harbour at Donaghadee (Montgomerie had acquired land in Down in 1605). The difficulties encountered in building and maintaining the harbours at Donaghadee and Portpatrick is a theme running through most of the last four centuries. The sorry tale requires its own space and provides the focus of the following chapter.

The recommendation came from Dublin Castle only after a commission had examined all possible sites along the coast between Strangford and Knockfergus Rivers. Donaghadee, the commission concluded, was the "only fittest place . . . for the saftie of boates, the good ease of passage, and the abilities of the towne for entertainemente of passengers".

The request was successful and the terms of the letters patent were that Montgomerie would maintain at Donaghadee no fewer than sixteen "passage boats" of eight or ten tons apiece (When applied to ships, a ton or tun is usually a measure of space or capacity. Originally, a tun was the space occupied by a tun cask of wine. In more modern usage, a gross ton equals 100 cubic feet or 2.83 cubic metres). The recommended rates for the crossing (currency is sterling) are shown in Table 1.

Table 1: Rates recommended in 1616.

	In summer	In winter
To hire a boat	15/- (75p)	20/- (£1)
A horse & man	2/6 (12$\frac{1}{2}$p)	3/- (15p)
A horse	2/- (10p)	2/6 (12$\frac{1}{2}$p)
Man or woman	8d (3$\frac{1}{3}$p)	8d (3$\frac{1}{2}$p)
Cow or ox	1/6 (7$\frac{1}{2}$p)	2/1 (10p)

A boat was not obliged to leave port until the fares onboard totalled the equivalent of hiring the boat.

Montgomerie was to hire a clerk who would record the names of all passengers arriving or leaving Donaghadee. An oath of allegiance was required from any "suspitious" person and a record was to be kept of all goods and livestock passing through the port. The clerk would also collect 2d. from each passenger, while 1d. was levied on each animal and each packet passing through.

It is assumed throughout the 1616 document that the Scottish end of the route would be Portpatrick.

John Stevenson in his Two Centuries of Life in Down, 1600-1800, speaks to the new traffic crossing the channel caused by the move of Scottish plantationers to Down and nearby areas. A contemporary report observes that "they [the Irish] hate the Scottyshe deadly" and so there was an incentive to keep in contact with the folks back home. Even one of the settlers described his fellow-settlers from England and Scotland as "generally the scum of the earth". Stevenson records that by 1607 it was not uncommon for Scots, when the weather was favourable, to go on horseback from Stranraer to Portpatrick with wares for sale, cross in a passage boat, hire horses at Donaghadee, ride to Newtownards (where Hugh Montgomerie had moved into the old castle), sell their produce in the market, reverse the journey, and be home the same day.

In addition to the matters of land ownership, kinship, and commercial links, religious and military elements created traffic passing through Portpatrick. The seventeenth century in Ireland witnessed an ongoing tussle between the episcopal and "non-conforming" (mainly presbyterian) parties. In the 1630s, the Episcopal Church of Ireland had the upper hand and many presbyterian ministers from Down took themselves off to Scotland. One, the Rev. Livingston, accepted a call to a congregation in Stranraer. Some of his Down congregation followed him while, we are told, twice a year a large group would cross from Donaghadee to Portpatrick to travel to Stranraer to participate in the communion service conducted by Mr. Livingston. It is recorded that one such group numbered five hundred while on one occasion he baptized 28 children brought over from Down.

During the short-lived Commonwealth period, especially in the late 1650s, the tide turned and many presbyterian clergy returned to Ulster, several receiving stipends from the government despite the inclination of some to pray openly for Charles II! (Charles had been crowned king of Scotland in 1651). Nothing is straightforward in the ecclesiastical history of Scotland and Ireland and further religious strife followed the Restoration Settlement of 1660 when Charles II moved to impose bishops on the Scottish presbyterians.

Foreshadowing civil war in England, rebellion broke out in Ulster in 1641. London, not without some misgivings, accepted the offer from the Scottish parliament to send 10,000 troops to Ulster. The force sailed from Ayrshire to Carrickfergus, Antrim, in February 1642 where the garrison was handed over to them. A considerable flow of refugees fleeing the conflict crossed to south-west Scotland. At this time, fear of privateers to the south caused Westminster to send all dispatches for Ireland via Portpatrick.

The military presence in Ireland caused the Scottish Privy Council to declare that the facilities for sending military dispatches between Edinburgh and Ireland had to be improved. In the first of many attempts at providing a reliable means of transportation for official dispatches, mail and travellers through Portpatrick, the Council in September 1642, set in motion plans for establishing postal stages between Edinburgh and Portpatrick. Work was to be done on the road between Dumfries and Portpatrick to bring it up to the grade of a "military road". John McCaig was appointed post-master at Portpatrick and received the standard annual stipend of £50 sterling. McCaig was instructed by the Council to obtain a "post bark". In the growing confusion of the times, it is hardly surprising to note that this attempt to establish a regular service did not last long.

In August 1662, yet another attempt was made to establish a reliable service between Portpatrick and Donaghadee. The Scottish Privy Council instructed Robert Mein (or Main), Keeper of the Letter Office at Edinburgh, to get a boat built to go "betwixt Portpatrik and

Dannachadie". Mein was to receive a commission of six shillings (Scottish = 2.5p) for each letter going to Ireland and £400 sterling annually. Mein contracted with Thomas Barins of Portpatrick to sail weekly with the mail to Donaghadee. Barins was allowed to take any passengers who turned up.

Mein was given a monopoly of mail going from Scotland to Ireland but the system was porous and soon abandoned. In May 1667, the Privy Council received a demand from Charles II that the route between Edinburgh and Ireland be re-established. A committee was set up but it was November 1677 before plans were announced to replace the foot-post on the Edinburgh-Portpatrick route with a horse post. Part of the plan instructed the postmaster at Portpatrick to keep a boat available for a twice-weekly crossing. The Scottish Parliament set aside £150 for the purchase of a boat.

How long this arrangement survived is not known. Certainly, in 1685, the Earl of Clarendon, Lord-Lieutenant of Ireland, wrote to London explaining that he intended to establish a packet boat between Ireland and Scotland. He complained that letters from Ireland to Edinburgh travelled by way of London.

The "Glorious Revolution" of 1688 when James II was deposed resulted in the postmaster at Portpatrick being instructed once again to ensure that a boat was available to carry mail to Ireland. A major interest on the part of the Scottish Privy Council was to maintain links with the William and Mary commander, the Duke of Schomberg, who had landed with 10,000 men on the Down shore of Belfast Lough. The military movements through Portpatrick were now of a frequency to justify the basing of three sloops at Portpatrick. When not required for military work, the sloops could be hired for a crossing and when engaged on official business would also take passengers on a space-available basis (From the early days of the plantations, the uncertainty of travel attaching to the route led to the building of substantial barracks at both Portpatrick and Donaghadee. The barracks at Portpatrick were originally in buildings formerly serving as a hostel for pilgrims, no doubt rendered redundant by the Reformation, but in 1800 a new barracks was built).

An act of parliament of 1695 made arrangements for a weekly mail crossing while the 1711 Post Office Act mandated a daily service between Portpatrick and Donaghadee. But difficulties continued and in 1759 no-one could be found to operate the mail contract and the Post Office was forced to fill the gap with its own boat and employees. Work on remaking the military road from Dumfries to Portpatrick had commenced in 1757 and by early 1759 had advanced sufficiently to allow its

EXPEDITIOUS TRAVELLING

FROM

LONDON TO GLASGOW AND PORTPATRICK,

IN FOUR DAYS,

BY WAY OF CARLISLE AND DUMFRIES.

A NEW POST COACH sets out from the 'CROSS KEYS,' WOOD STREET, LONDON, *every evening* (Saturday excepted), and arrives at BECK'S COFFEE HOUSE, CARLISLE, in three days ; also sets out from BECK'S COFFEE HOUSE, CARLISLE, *on the same evening*, and arrives in three days at the 'CROSS KEYS,' LONDON. To accommodate passengers travelling northward and to Ireland A NEW POST COACH, which connects with the above, sets out from 'KING'S ARMS HOTEL,' CARLISLE, *every Tuesday and Thursday morning* at six o'clock for DUMFRIES ; upon arrival of which at the 'GEORGE INN,' a DILIGENCE sets out for GLASGOW and another for PORTPATRICK: Also a DILIGENCE sets out from MR. BUCHANAN'S, the 'SARACEN'S HEAD,' GLASGOW, and another from MR. CAMPBELL'S, PORTPATRICK, *every Tuesday and Thursday morning* at four o'clock, to join the said DUMFRIES AND CARLISLE POST COACH, in which seats will be reserved for those travelling southward.

Each inside passenger from Carlisle to Glasgow or Portpatrick to pay £1 16s. 6d., and to be allowed ten pounds weight of luggage ; all above to pay 2d. per lb. Children on the lap to pay half-price. Insides from Carlisle to Dumfries to pay 11s. 8d.; outsides, 6s. 8d. Small parcels from Carlisle to Portpatrick or Glasgow to pay 1s. 6d. each ; all upwards of nine pounds to pay 2d. per pound Passengers taken up on the road to pay 4d. per mile in both the Coach and Diligence; and for outsides on the Coach 2½d. per mile. Insides from London to Glasgow, £3 6s. Ditto from Carlisle to Glasgow or Portpatrick, £1 16s. 6d. Total : London to Glasgow or Portpatrick, £5 2s. 6d.

Coaching poster for 1779.

use by coaches (Another ten years would elapse before the road was completed. The importance of the Portpatrick route is indicated by this road being the only military road constructed outside the Highlands).

While maintaining a regular communication for the mail was a continual struggle, the use of the route by individuals continued. When John Wesley's itinerant preaching took him to Portpatrick in April 1765, his party received many offers for transportation across to Ireland. But with the wind being "full in our teeth", there was a day's delay before the crossing could be made. Wesley confided in his diary, "It seemed strange to cross the sea in an open boat, especially when the waves ran high. I was a little sick, till I fell asleep. In five and a half hours we reached Donaghadee". Wesley's return trip was by way of Dublin and Whitehaven, but lack of ships at both Bristol and Liverpool forced Wesley back to Portpatrick in late March 1767. He crossed to Donaghadee in three hours. Wesley returned to Donaghadee in late August but found all the Post Office packet boats were on the Scottish side and he had to negotiate with the captain of a "small boat" to be taken over to Portpatrick.

An affair of the heart brought James Boswell to Portpatrick two years later when, in May 1769, Boswell and his cousin hired the services of a boat for the crossing to Ireland. Boswell knew sickness was well nigh inevitable and hoped by sailing late in the day that he could sleep. Anyway, he concluded, the boat had a good cabin. He was indeed sick for much of the five-hour crossing: "I tried to brave it out for a while, but grew very sick". Boswell remarked, as many still do, "It was pleasant to see the Irish coast".

Around this time another trade began to take on importance. By the 1760s, England was finding it increasingly difficult to feed its people and the farmers of Ireland were quick to develop a supply of black cattle. The volume of livestock passing through Portpatrick had been increasing steadily from 1765 when a hundred-year ban on importing cattle and horses was lifted. Earlier in the century the Navy had patrolled the Irish Sea in order to enforce a wide range of restrictions of exports from Ireland. In fact much of the history of English-Irish relations in the eighteenth century revolves around Irish demands for "free trade" and England's concern for protecting its merchants. In 1702, fears at Westminster over evasion of the bans caused the Admiralty to inform its commanders that "the usual port in the north where this offense is frequently practised is Donaghadee, over against Portpatrick in Scotland. Take particular care of the port of Donaghadee".

In 1779-80 most of the restrictions on Irish exports and imports were removed and trade began to grow slowly. We are reminded that part of the context of this easing of trade restrictions was the American

Revolution then underway — a fight which had trade at its heart. France was providing support for the colonies seeking independence and there was fear in London of French troops landing in Ireland. In April 1778, the weakness of the British Navy in home waters was demonstrated when the American privateer *Ranger*, under the command of John Paul Jones, a son of Kirkcudbrightshire, made several successful raids on the coast of England and Scotland. Jones then sailed into Belfast Lough where he had his way with merchant shipping as well as HM sloop *Drake*. The mail route through Portpatrick was under threat and on Friday, 1st May, 1778, HM sloop *Thetis* sailed from Greenock for Portpatrick to give some protection to the mail.

A 1778 map reminds us of the importance of Donaghadee to communications within Ireland. Taylor and Skinner's Maps of the Roads of Ireland devotes its first ten pages to the two roads linking Dublin and Donaghadee, one via Portaferry and the other via Newtownards. Belfast is shown incidentally as one of several towns through which the latter road passes.

An extract from the Belfast Newsletter of 2nd May, 1783, gives an indication of the mail traffic passing between Donaghadee and Portpatrick.

Donaghadee Port Intelligence

Arrivals

April

24. The *Sisters*, with the [mail] packet and passengers
    The *Fortune*, with merchant goods from Glasgow
25. The *Kilwarlin*, with the Right Hon. Mr. Winfield, and other passengers
26. The *Dublin,* with passengers
27. The *Yacht*, with Major Savage, and others
28. The *Sisters*, with the packet and Geo. Fullerton, Esq., Collector of Leith
29. The *Kilwarlin*, with the packet and passengers
30. The *Sisters*, with the packet and passengers

Sailed

22. The *Kilwarlin*, with the packet and passengers
    The *Dublin*, with passengers
23. The *James and Mary*
24. The *Kilwarlin*, with the packet and passengers
25. The *Sisters*, with the packet and passengers
26. The *Kilwarlin*, with the packet, Mr Fulton of Coleraine, Mr. Richardson of Berwick on Tweed, and several other passengers
27. The *Sisters*, with the packet, Major Knox, and Miss Forde
    The *Dublin*, with passengers
28. The *Kilwarlin*, with the packet and passengers
    The *Yacht*, with Samuel Jameson, Esq., and lady

29. The *Sisters*, with the packet and passengers
    Two Sloops in ballast, for Whitehaven
    The *Kyle*, with passengers, for Douglas

While the expansion of trade allowed after the 1779-80 relaxation was slow, the carriage of livestock continued to grow and in 1790 over 17,000 beasts were carried across to Portpatrick. The combination of black cattle and passengers on the small sailing ships must have produced conditions far from ideal.

It was in 1790 that a fine customs house was built at Portpatrick. The building is now the Harbour House Hotel. For part of the nineteenth century it was the home of the Admiralty's superintendent at Portpatrick.

While trade through Portpatrick and Donaghadee appeared set to continue its growth, domestic strife was an ever-present threat. Fears of a French invasion of Ireland remained alive for a couple of decades, indeed the leaders of the United Irishmen's insurrection of 1798 were counting on it. But in the event, Bonaparte found Egypt more appealing than Ireland and the French troops when they reached Kilala, Mayo, in August 1798 were too little too late. The insurrection lasted only a matter of months but its ferocity in Ulster closed down the Portpatrick route for several weeks in June and July 1798. A "passport" system was introduced briefly, and an interesting survivor is reproduced nearby.

John Stevenson closes his Two Centuries of Life in Down, 1600-1800, with extracts from the diary of Anne, Dowager Countess of Roden, whose family was caught up in the insurrection. The family set out at daybreak on Friday, June 8th, 1798, from Tollymore in Down for Belfast to join those fleeing across to Scotland. On the Saturday they joined a coal boat, *Liberty*, part of a total cargo of 53 women and children. "The ship was wonderfully crowded", the Countess recorded in her diary. The Countess's suspicions as to the intentions of the pilot were heightened when two low tides were spent ashore on separate shoals in the River Lagan. But Portpatrick was reached safely in the late afternoon of Monday, 11th June.

"When we landed, the town of Portpatrick was so completely full of military going to Ireland, and fugitives from thence, that we had no hopes of a bed of any kind: we could only get a dirty bed-chamber in the inn to eat our dinner".

The Countess eventually was accommodated in the manse of the parish minister, Rev. John McKenzie (see below), before continuing

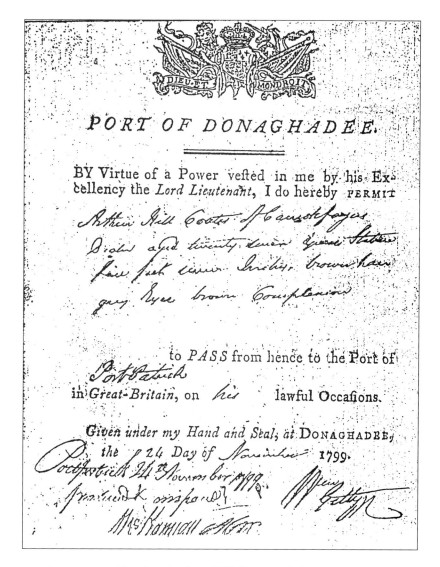

A passport allowing Arthur Hill Coates of Carrickfergus to pass from Donaghadee to Portpatrick on 24th November 1799. On the reverse side, the passport is endorsed, "Permit the bearer to return to Donaghadee 29th December 1799".

on her way to Longtown, some 28 miles east of Dumfries. After the insurrection petered out, the Countess returned, leaving Portpatrick on September 19th for Donaghadee and on to her home at Tollymore.

While the insurrection was short-lived, it cast a long shadow over Irish affairs and led to the Act of Union implemented in 1801 when the Irish Parliament was disbanded and all legislature handled by the parliament in Westminster.

The multi-volume (first) Statistical Account of Scotland began to appear in 1791. Penned by Church of Scotland ministers it gives a parish-by-parish window into life at the time. In volume 1, the Rev. John McKenzie, who in June 1798 came to the rescue of the Dowager Countess of Roden (see above), describes the situation at Portpatrick's harbour. He recalls that the lack of an adequate harbour until recently had dictated the use of flat-bottomed boats, "flats", on the route since they had to be run on to the shore at both ends of the crossing.

"The whole inhabitants, men and women, ran down and by main force, dragged [the flat] up the beach, out of the reach of the waves. These were times of misery, but the inhabitants were the happiest of mortals. Their continued exertions in launching and drawing up their vessels, excited wonderful spirits, which they knew how to recruit when exhausted. Every day that a vessel sailed or arrived was a festival".

Rev. McKenzie could remember a time when a regular sailing packet service was supposed to operate for the mail and passengers. The frequent delays were, he recalled, possibly related to the practice of paying the wages whether or not the ships sailed. He noted with a sigh that it was only natural that "the sailors often chose to rest themselves". The service was so erratic that soon payment for carrying the mail was made to any packet that was prepared to cross.

The parish minister relates another less attractive side of Portpatrick.

"At this, as well as at every ferry or passage, there are a set of people who make themselves useful to passengers, but who distinguish themselves also by the impositions which they practice. There are about twenty persons of that description at Portpatrick, who are known by the name of the Robbery, from their supposed depredations of the public. They are absolutely necessary at this port; and another body of the same sort are equally serviceable at the other side of the channel; but the manner in which their fees are exacted, particularly when they meet with any difficulty in the payment, is rather harsh and disagreeable".

Rev. McKenzie identified John Palmer of the Post Office as the individual responsible for bringing some order back to the short sea crossing. Palmer had greatly improved the reliability of the movement of mail by establishing a network of mail coaches in England. Portpatrick was still a major link between England and the north of Ireland and as a result of Palmer's work, a mail coach began operating between Dumfries and Portpatrick in 1790 (In 1805, a coach was put in service between Edinburgh and Portpatrick, via Dumfries). In 1791, the Post Office went one step further and entered into a contract for a daily packet service with a firm headed by the Marquis of Downshire. The Donaghadee Packet Company provided four Thames-built ships for a daily service for the mail and in return received an annual fee of £700, increased to £925 in 1821 and £1,000 a year later. McKenzie described the ships, *Hillsborough*, *Palmer*, *Downshire*, and *Westmoreland*, as "elegant vessels fitted with every accommodation". Each boat had a crew of six. The agents at Donaghadee, a Mr. Lemon, and at Portpatrick, a Mr. Hannay, plus the ships' masters, were each obliged to invest £50 in the company. The company kept all revenue earned from the conveyance of passengers and cargo. Rev. McKenzie noted with some satisfaction that two of the "flats" had been abandoned on the shore at Portpatrick "as monuments of an ancient barbarity". In an attempt to address the ancient barbarity, the mail packets were not allowed to carry livestock.

The carriage of livestock continued to grow. The experience of one traveller in December 1796 is worth reporting "The number of cattle taken from [Donaghadee] to Scotland is something inconceivable. On the day I crossed there were four hundred horned cattle taken over to Scotland, and in the six weeks previous there had been transported nearly thirty thousand. The farmers are obliged to submit to the impudent impositions of the owners of the boats which take the cattle. They ask as much as twenty guineas (£21) for a crossing; and as they hold the farmer in the hollow of their hand he is obliged to pay what they ask, and this means that the cost . . . is as much as one guinea (£1.05) per beast".

The traveller, a Frenchman by the name of de Latocnaye, discovered another "trade". He observed that illegitimate children were often sent over to Ireland for baptism while the lower age in Scotland for marriage without parental consent brought young couples to Ireland's "Gretna Green" at Portpatrick. De Latocnaye made the crossing to Portpatrick in the fast time of $2^1/_2$ hours. He was less fortunate on his return journey when he was tossed about for 13 hours. Records also survive of crossings measured in days rather than hours and sometimes the travellers would find themselves driven back to their starting point. The uncertainty of the crossing and the relative isolation of both ports brought a degree of prosperity to the harbour villages as would-be travellers were forced to find accommodation for days or even weeks, "waiting for the wind" - one observer commented that "almost every house is an inn." There were times when expediency or impatience required that passengers and the mail were rowed across. Finally, it must be noted that "the start was not, with high degree of certainty, followed by finish at the desired haven."

An invitation in 1819 to submit bids for the conveyance of the mail between Belfast and Donaghadee.

2. BUILDING THE HARBOURS

In 1620, Sir Hugh Montgomerie, already established as the plantationer in Donaghadee, Co. Down, purchased the Barony (or land) of Portree which included the harbour at Portpatrick. In 1616, Montgomerie had been granted letters patent giving him the ferry rights for the Donaghadee-Portpatrick passage. Montgomerie set about constructing a quay at Donaghadee and this harbour was completed by 1626. The harbour would remain basically unaltered for 150 years and W. Harris (The Ancient and Present State of the County of Down, 1744) described it thus:

"The quay at Donaghadee is made of large stones in the form of a crescent, without any cement, and 128 yards in length and about 20 to 22 feet broad, besides a breast wall of the same kind of stones about six feet broad".

In 1775, the owner of the quay, Daniel Delacherois, petitioned the Irish Parliament for £1,500 towards the repair of the quay. He was granted only £1,000 but soon found that a complete rebuilding of the harbour was necessary. A further grant of £1,705 was made towards the work and by 1785 the quay had been extended by some thirty feet and the harbour inside the crescent had a depth of five feet at low tide.

While Donaghadee had a rudimentary harbour by the 1620s, it was almost another hundred years before an attempt was made to improve on nature at Portpatrick. A 1716 document has survived which reflects an agreement between James Anderson, deputy postmaster general of Scotland, and John Blair of Dunskey in which the latter undertakes to continue work on constructing a quay at Portpatrick. This quay, to be completed by the first day of August 1717, would be able to accommodate three packet boats of 14 tons capacity.

No record survives of what this structure looked like. At that time and considering the size of the ships, a quay might be no more elaborate than a loose construction of boulders of modest height built out into the bay. Or, it could have been the beginnings of what later in the century was referred to as the "platform" alongside one of the rocks on the north-east corner of the bay.

In the 1760s, the military road between Dumfries and Portpatrick was being remade and the British Parliament appropriated funds for the improvement of the harbour at Portpatrick. John Smeaton, of Eddystone Lighthouse fame, was asked to make recommendations. In October 1768, he visited Portpatrick and reported that

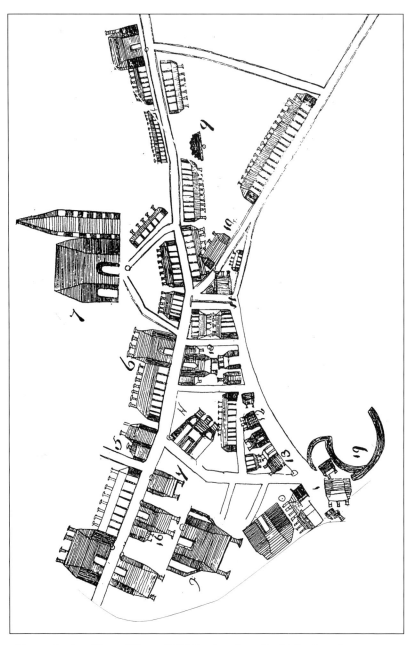

Donaghadee Town Plan of 1780, showing the Delacherois quay as Number 19.

he found the harbour "entirely in a state of nature, a small platform for the more commodious landing and shipping of passengers, &c. excepted". Vessels would come alongside the platform and be left high and dry at low tide. Thinking of sailing vessels of up to 40-ton capacity, Smeaton was impressed with the natural advantages of the harbour: ease of access and egress, sufficient depth even at low tide for vessels to remain afloat, some protection from storms from seven-eighths of the compass. He concluded that it would be sufficient to provide protection against storms from the south through south-west.

Because of the exposure of the harbour, the ships using Portpatrick had to be of a design that allowed them to be driven on the sandy beach in the harbour. That meant they had to be flat-bottomed. This in turn required that to make the passage to Donaghadee, the wind had to be on the beam, i.e. from a northerly or southerly direction and balanced by a countervailing tide current. Any other combination of wind and tide would cause the ships to make leeway and force them many miles off the correct course.

Smeaton reasoned that if extra protection were to be provided at Portpatrick the ships would not need to be driven on the shore and so could be of a design less dependent on a favourable combination of wind and tide to make the crossing.

Smeaton's plan for Portpatrick involved constructing this protection by building on the south side only of the harbour. The construction consisted of a hub with three unequal spokes. The hub was close to where the lighthouse keeper's house is today and the first spoke, running at "eight o'clock" filled in the "south gullet" between the shore and the east end of St. Catherine's Isle which formed the natural south side of the harbour. It was 120 feet long, roughly 18 feet high, 32 feet wide at the base tapering to 18 feet at the top. The spoke running at "twelve o'clock" was constructed along the spine of St. Catherine's Isle and was to be 400 feet long. It was built on the rock and averaged 10 feet in height and had a 24 feet wide base tapering to 18 feet. This spoke finished with a 40 foot long head turned to face north-west which Smeaton was confident would greatly increase the protection within the harbour without diminishing the area. These two spokes were jointly referred to as the exterior pier. The spoke running at "four o'clock" was the interior pier and was the only part of the structure along which ships could lie. The interior pier was curved towards the north-east, again to provide maximum shelter without interfering with the area of the harbour and also to minimise the effect of waves reflected off the wall of the pier. This spoke was to be 180 feet in length. The exterior pier had a parapet, 6 feet high and 3 feet wide, running along the exposed side, while the parapet on the interior pier was to be 4 feet high. The exterior pier would take the brunt of any storms and so the interior pier was only 15 feet wide and was raised only 4 feet above high water mark compared with 6 feet for the exterior pier.

Additionally, Smeaton planned to smooth off more of the face of the rock upon which or alongside which the old platform was found and extend the size of the platform itself. He proposed to place some timber facing on the rock to improve further the usefulness of the platform. In order to reduce the danger to ships manoeuvring or lying at anchor in the harbour, Smeaton proposed to blast some rocks down to the level of the sandy beach. Smeaton's primary objective was to provide protection for ships of up to 40 tons which were either at anchor in the harbour, alongside the platform, or drawn up on the beach, and he debated with himself where the obstruction caused by the interior pier would outweigh the benefits from the protection provided.

The tops and outer surface of the piers were to be constructed from rock quarried and chiselled into somewhat of a square shape. Smeaton could find no suitable stone in the area and he surmised it would need to be brought in by sea. In the event it came from Anglesey. The infilling of the piers could be adequately handled with rough stones readily available around the harbour at Portpatrick. Smeaton's estimated cost was £5,802.16/6d. (£5,802.82$\frac{1}{2}$p.)

Towards the end of 1773, the pier had been built across the south gullet and work had started on the second spoke along St. Catherine's Isle when Smeaton decided to stop work on the exterior pier for the moment and start on the interior pier (One wonders if he had been subjected to impatience from the Post Office). The design of the interior pier had to be modified since it would now bear the full brunt of the storms. Previously to be curved, the pier was now straight. It was heightened to be 6 feet above the high water mark and widened to 18 feet across the top while the parapet was increased to 8 feet. A round stone pillar was placed at the extremity of the parapet and it was Smeaton's intention that a flag or lantern could be placed there. The flag could be used, he suggested, to indicate the depth of water inside the pier. A substantial stone bollard was placed beyond the pillar and was to be used by ships being warped in and out of the harbour. A set of stairs was built just inside the head of the pier which would allow passengers to be landed at any state of the tide by boats from ships lying in the harbour. Smeaton took a few feet off the length of the pier to ensure 100 feet of clearance between the end of the pier and the platform rock.

Smeaton intended that the exterior pier would be completed once the interior pier was operational but in the event work was never resumed and the west end of the exterior pier remained a short stump.

By 1790, a lighthouse had been built on this stump. It was

described as a revolving timber lighthouse and appears to have been used only when a mail packet was expected (General shipping continued to depend on a light burning in the gable-end window of one of the houses). In the 1850s, a writer to the Galloway Advertiser recalled his grandfather's stories of when he was custodian of this early lighthouse. His grandfather mentioned that the lantern shutters were revolved through gearing by a system of ropes, one of which had loops spaced along its length at prescribed distances and on to these a water-filled leather bucket was attached as the rope made its vertical descent. As the bucket reached the bottom of its travel another bucket was attached at the top and the lower one hastily removed ere the rope began its upward climb. A tank filled with sea water supplied the ballast for the buckets. The lighthouse keeper would surely have to be nimble to keep going up and down the ladder! The grandson tells us that it was a messy job and his grandfather soon substituted stones for the water. Initially, tallow candles were the means of illumination, but oil soon took over.

One observer was driven to conclude, "The lighthouse is particularly useful, and as there has long been another lighthouse on the Irish side, it renders the passage, even in the darkest night, convenient and comfortable, like a street well-lighted on both sides".

On the "Irish side", a beacon had been constructed in the eighteenth century on the Copeland Islands off Donaghadee. The Dublin Ballast Board was created in 1810 and given responsibility for Irish lighthouses. Reflecting the importance attached to the harbour, the board's first new lighthouse was completed on one of the Copeland Islands.

The ingenuity of even John Smeaton was not equal to the strength of an angry sea at Portpatrick and on at least two occasions, in 1786 and 1792, the interior pier was badly damaged in storms. On both occasions a bulwark was constructed on the outside wall of the pier but the solution failed. The desperate expedient was adopted of simply piling up boulders along the outside face of the pier but succeeded only in providing boulders for the seas to push into the main harbour.

In 1801, the engineer John Rennie was brought in to look at the harbour and he expressed concern over the bulwark which did not seem to be holding. He suggested that oak fenders be placed round the head of the pier since the pier was being damaged by ships striking it (One must assume that in these encounters with the rough stone surface the ships usually came off the losers).

While Smeaton's pier would be superseded, a stump of the interior pier, anchored well into the rock, did remain standing up to the 1990s as a reminder of that engineering genius of the eighteenth century.

Events, domestic and international, combined to underline the importance and the inadequacy of the link between Portpatrick and Donaghadee. The Act of Union became effective in 1801 and removed the Irish Parliament. Now legislation for Ireland was handled at Westminster while Dublin Castle remained the seat of government. The amount of mail communication between Ireland and the rest of the United Kingdom increased significantly as did commerce.

In 1809, a select committee at Westminster received a report from the engineer, Thomas Telford. Telford concurred with Smeaton's design and positioning of the pier at Portpatrick: "The pier having been placed in a very judicious manner, vessels are very secure when once got fairly into the harbour", but heargued that reliability of the crossing would be greatly increased if a back-up route was developed. He suggested that harbours be built at Portlogan (Portnessock, as it was then called), some miles south of Portpatrick, and at Bangor, Co. Down, north-west of Donaghadee (Bangor's small harbour was already supporting a sizeable livestock trade to Workington and Portpatrick).

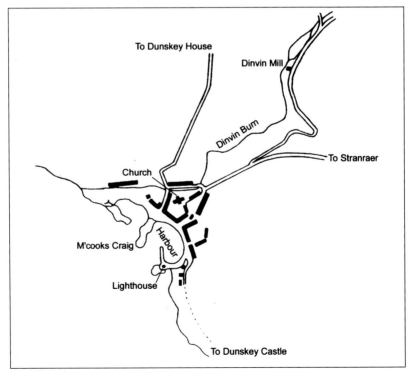

Portpatrick in 1808.

Telford argued for a separate packet operator for the Bangor route to ensure competition for the Donaghadee Packet Company. If both routes were available not only would the crossing be less weather-dependent but the pressure of competition would further improve the quality of the service offered to passengers and the mail.

Lord Cathcart, Commander of the Forces in Scotland, offered his support for Telford's recommendations, especially the use of Bangor. Cathcart's first preference as the Scottish port was Ardrossan where a harbour had been built to Telford's design. Portlogan he considered a good secondary port which could also be served from Bangor. No doubt, Cathcart's views were influenced by his experience in January and February 1806 when it required over five weeks to transport a troop of the 7th Dragoon Guards from Portpatrick to Donaghadee.

The treasurer of the Donaghadee Packet Company, Edward Hull, was successful in his vehement defence of Donaghadee-Portpatrick as the sole mail route. While Telford's recommendation on the use of Portlogan and Bangor was rejected, the government did approve his plans for the improvement of the harbour at Portpatrick. The pier required strengthening and a new wall of squared masonry about five feet thick was built along the outside of the pier. Also, cement was applied to the original dry-stone structure.

Telford had seen first hand in 1802 the conditions at Portpatrick when the wind was from the west. He had embarked on the mail packet *Palmer* for Donaghadee and it took two hours to clear the harbour at Portpatrick. Telford relates the process employed. Two boats were rowed out of the harbour into the breaking seas; one carried a heavy anchor attached to about 250 fathoms (1,500 feet) of rope in the other boat. The other end of the rope was held on the *Palmer*. Once well clear of the harbour and at the limit of the rope, the anchor was dropped and the packet pulled and tacked its way out of the harbour and off the shore.

Disputes over the best routes were ongoing. An alternative with advocates was Larne to Cairnryan. Larne Lough provided a good anchorage but, in the days of sailing ships, the Maidens Islands off the lough's entrance were a cause for concern. Debate over the best route was behind the request made in 1817 to John Rennie to present a report to the Post Office on the topic. In his work, Rennie received the help of Trinity House and in February 1819 his report duly reached the Postmaster General. Trinity House came down in favour of Portpatrick and Donaghadee as the "two most eligible places for packet stations".

Rennie provided plans for improvement of the harbours at Portpatrick and Donaghadee. His plans were accompanied by a statement of support signed by the masters of the mail packets and several other vessels plying between the ports. John Rennie's plans were approved. With hindsight it is interesting to note that Donaghadee was expected to be the more costly at £140,633 compared with £115,280 for Portpatrick. Also, today we find Donaghadee Harbour almost exactly as Rennie planned it two centuries ago (except that a rather grand entry arch was never built), while at Portpatrick the relentless working of the sea has left only traces of his work.

Several factors guided Rennie in his plans, especially at Portpatrick. The ideal time for a sailing ship to leave Portpatrick for Donaghadee was at the beginning of the flood or ebb, depending on the prevailing wind. The ships would be afloat within the harbour at Portpatrick at the beginning of the ebb, but could well be aground at the beginning of the flood since lying on the beach was often the only means of sheltering. So, he argued, the harbour had to allow the ships to be both afloat and sheltered at all times. Rennie designed his harbours to provide the maximum room for manoeuvring with the maximum shelter. The former allowed the ships to tack while still in the harbour and the latter meant the ships could lie alongside the quays without sustaining damage caused by surging against the quay wall. The general design Rennie used at Portpatrick, Donaghadee and elsewhere was to build two piers out into the sea and with short heads, or "jetties", turned in to provide a narrow entrance.

Rennie argued that the jetties would not only increase the shelter inside the harbour but also the rebound of the seas from the outer corners of the jetties would force approaching ships into the channel and minimize the chances of a ship colliding with the piers as it entered.

At Donaghadee, John Rennie came to the conclusion that "It does not seem to me that anything effectual can be done on a moderate scale". Instead of trying to improve the Delacherois harbour, Rennie's plans called for a completely new structure.

The south pier was built outward from the landward end of Delacherois' quay for 430 feet along a rock base, plus three angled sections, or cants, each of approximately 100 feet length. The north pier, at a total length of some 800 feet was built over the Little and Great Dulce Rocks which had acted as natural breakwaters for the old quay. Unlike the south pier, the north pier was not connected to the shore (except at low tide when the landward end dried out). Both piers shared the feature of angled sections inclining towards each other and so while the harbour was some 550 feet wide, the entrance was only about 140 feet in width. Rock was removed from within the harbour and this allowed for between 14 and 16 feet of water at low tide. The

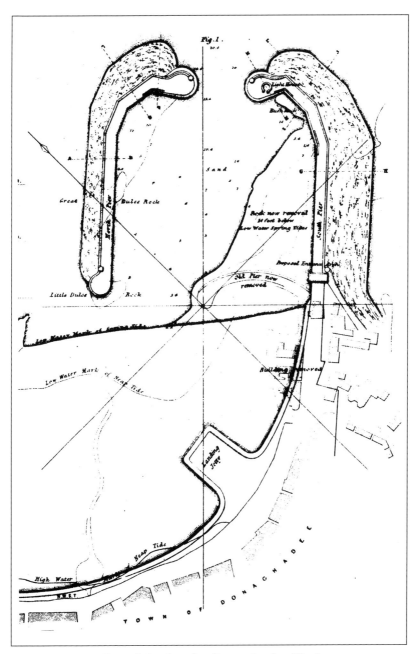

John Rennie's plan for Donaghadee Harbour.

inner faces of both piers were finished to allow ships to berth alongside. Material blasted off the rocks and floor of the harbour was used in the piers' construction, but the ashlar masonry of limestone was transported from quarries worked by convicts at Moelfre on the north-west coast of Anglesey.

The first stone at Donaghadee was laid by the Marquis of Downshire on 1st August 1821. Shortly thereafter, John Rennie died and it fell to his son, John Jr, to see the plans through to fruition and to experience the parsimonious manner in which the Treasury released the funds. This fiscal practice dictated that the work proceed at a leisurely rate and it was 1837 before the construction at Donaghadee was really completed. By 1823, however, the Marquis of Downshire, head of the Donaghadee Packet Company, considered the work sufficiently advanced to appeal to Dublin Castle for steam packets to be placed on the route. The Packet Company investigated possible steamships, but were not encouraged to proceed. Donaghadee harbour commissioners, appointed in 1824, met for the last time in December 1837 when responsibility for the harbour was transferred to the Irish Board of Public Works.

On Saturday, 21st May, 1825, the sea was readmitted to what was identified as the "outer basin" of the harbour at Donaghadee. The previous evening a celebration was held on the floor of the harbour "which never after was to be trodden by the foot of man". Eleven men sat down to a meal under the chairmanship of Harbour Master Lemon and several toasts were proposed. The Belfast Newsletter reported that the scene "had something of an awful or solemn appearance, being sur-rounded within an immense mass of waters".

At Portpatrick, Rennie followed his usual design of having two piers stretching out to sea and angled towards each other to provide the maximum area inside with the minimum exposure consistent with a safe entrance. The end result would have been of horseshoe shape. The south pier was carried out in a south-west direction along St Catherine's Isle in a manner similar to Smeaton's original design but Rennie called for a structure of greater dimensions and more substantial construction. The pier was 500 feet in length with a jetty 80 feet long and 30 feet wide at right angles to the inner face of the pier. Rocks would be blasted to allow ships to lie alongside the northern face of the pier. A substantial and elegant lighthouse was to be placed at the end of the south pier (An almost identical structure was built on the south pier at Donaghadee). To the north, a pier, 800 feet long, was to run out at an angle to the shore, passing to the north-west of McCook's Craig, a massive rock. The space between the north pier and the Craig was to be filled in. Like the south pier, the head of the north pier had a jetty pointing into the harbour. The entrance between the piers was to be about 180 feet wide. Rennie expected the mail packets to be able to lie alongside either the north or south piers in the shelter provided by the jetties. They would be afloat at all times.

Once work started in 1821, Portpatrick was transformed. One

Donaghadee lighthouse.

visitor recorded in Fullerton's Gazette that suddenly:

"In place of a few fishermen lounging about and wondering why the herring have not arrived, you see 800 able-bodied men whose labours are . . . triumphing over the most formidable obstacles of nature".

John MacDiarmid, the Dumfries journalist, reflecting on the work embarked on in 1821, wrote in Sketches from Nature published in 1830, "To obtain a faint idea of the bustle and animation that prevailed at Port Patrick a few years ago, the reader must picture to himself from seven to eight hundred labourers, digging, building, quarrying — trundling the barrow, handling the spade — to say nothing of a host of carpenters and blacksmiths — some erecting cranes, cranks, scaffolds — some keeping up the tear and wear of the system, and not a few engaged in repairing and sharpening the numerous tools which others were constantly employed in blunting. Altogether, a visit to Port Patrick serves to elevate our conception of human ingenuity".

A tramway was constructed to carry stone from a quarry south of the village. The stone was taken to the Admiralty yard to the north of the harbour. Stone was also brought from Dunbartonshire and Anglesey (The realignment of the shorefront to accommodate the tramway helps explain why some homes on the front at Portpatrick are now below street level). For a time, work on the harbour continued day and night. Even so, it was to be years before much was accomplished and, in fact, the project at Portpatrick was never finished.

By 1833, the south pier was completed and in 1836 the new lighthouse at its seaward end brought into use. Work continued on the north pier. On Sunday, 6th January, 1839, a severe north-westerly gale caused a breach in the south pier and the lighthouse was in danger of collapsing into the sea. The Treasury appropriated funds on a year-to-year basis and the money earmarked for work on the north pier had to be diverted to repair the south pier. The sea soon began dismantling the incomplete north pier and work on the pier was now abandoned and never resumed. Despite the work on the south pier, the lighthouse was taken out of commission and the older lighthouse brought back into use.

For the Dumfries journalist, the spectacle at Portpatrick was uplifting, but there was some regret locally with the work at the harbour. The Glasgow Herald in April 1824 reported:

"Though we are all delighted with the improvements that are going on, we regret the loss of a number of antiquities which time has rendered sacred in our eyes — the rock called the Old or St. Patrick's Kirk with the impression of the saint's foot three inches deep on it having yielded to the merciless attacks of boring irons and barrels of gunpowder. And his pole upon St. Catherine's from which he unloosed his barge when he set sail for that land — not of milk and honey but of potatoes and buttermilk — must soon give way to the same sacri-legious powers".

As at Donaghadee, a local board of harbour commissioners was appointed in 1820. Unlike Donaghadee, the commissioners' work at Portpatrick was never concluded and over the years some resigned as they realised the futility of the task confronting them. In 1847, the remaining commissioners petitioned successfully to have responsibility for the harbour transferred to the Admiralty. The Admiralty appointed Captain Edward Hawes as superintendent.

Portpatrick Harbour was never completed to Rennie's design and there was continual dissatisfaction with the reliability of the mail service even after steam packets were introduced in 1825 (see next chapter). Government committees would recommend abandonment in 1830, 1836 and 1842 but were ignored.

With the benefit of hindsight, it is doubtful if Portpatrick Harbour, even if completed, could have done the job. It was designed with sailing ships in mind and we must question John Rennie's claims, as late as 1842, that the original plans required no modification to accommodate steamships. According to Rennie, the needs of sailing ships and steamships were not markedly different, despite the latter being, by the 1840s, twice the size of the former. The claims were made before a Parliamentary Select committee appointed in 1842 to investigate Post Office Communications. The same committee heard from Captain George Evans, RN, who considered attempts to make Portpatrick Harbour safe as "a useless expense, just the same as throwing the money into the sea". But in 1849, the matter was temporarily put "on hold".

The mail service between Portpatrick and Donaghadee was ter-minated in July 1849 when the Post Office took up the offer from George Burns, a Glasgow shipowner, to carry the mail free between Greenock and Belfast. The establishment at Portpatrick was closed down by Captain Hawes and the harbour now saw only an occasional coastal sailing vessel. But local interests at both ends of the route lost no time in arguing for the re-establishment of the route since they were confident Burns would demand a substantial fee from the Post Office once he had them captive.

After much lobbying, the Treasury agreed in August 1856 to provide funds for further work at both harbours with a view to the mail route being re-opened. The difference now was that the harbours would be linked by rail to Belfast, Glasgow and, via Dumfries, the North of England and even London.

The Admiralty had Captain James Vetch, head of the Harbour Department, provide plans and estimates of the work at Portpatrick and Donaghadee. The harbour at Donaghadee was in good shape and now

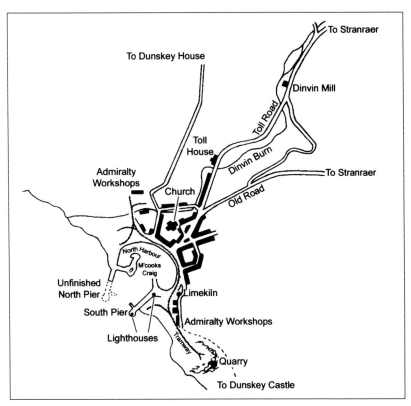

Portpatrick in 1840.

the responsibility of the Board of Public Works, Dublin. Captain Vetch agreed with the recommendation of Barry Gibbons, Harbour Engineer for the Board, that the principal need would be dredging, some rock blasting, and reinforcement of the outer sides of the two piers at a cost of £9,900 (There was some muttering that work had been left incomplete by Rennie). This estimate came in just below the Treasury's working figure of £10,000 and the matter was pretty well settled by late 1856. Gibbons borrowed a dredger ("dredging machine") from Galway and a diving bell from Kingstown (now Dun Laoghaire) and the work was completed within both the promised two years and the budget. The railway linking Donaghadee to Newtownards and so Belfast was opened for passenger traffic on the 3rd June, 1861.

Portpatrick was more of a challenge. The "temporary" mail berth in the north side of the harbour tucked in between McCook's Craig and the shore end of the north pier could barely accommodate the steam packets of 100 feet length. Captain James Vetch visited Portpatrick in September 1856 to develop a plan for the harbour that would allow for the larger mail packets operating in the 1850s. In June 1858, Vetch sent his proposal to the Admiralty to get Portpatrick Harbour into a usable state. His plans included completing the north pier, providing a channel to a new dock, north of the old mail berth. This dock would be able to accommodate steamships of up to 150 feet in length (Vetch accepted the model of two of the mail packets on the Folkestone-Boulogne route which were 144 feet in length and capable of completing the 26-mile crossing in two hours. For comparison, the Burns' ships sailing between Greenock and Belfast now exceeded 200 feet in length). Vetch estimated the cost as £30,000. The Admiralty passed Vetch's plans along to the Treasury but gave the estimated cost as £40,000, but indicated that £10,000 should be asked for during the 1858-59 parliament.

It did not take the Admiralty long to point out that the August 1856 agreement was based on an estimate for Portpatrick of a total of £15,000. The Admiralty was asked to have Vetch reconsider. He did, and by omitting work on completing the north pier, got the estimate down to £19,490. The Treasury accepted this.

Construction of the north pier had been abandoned in 1839 and by the 1840s the north pier was disintegrating, causing large blocks to become loose and drift into the main channel. In September 1846 a floating crane had been brought from Holyhead to lift stones toppled from the north pier. Vetch continued this work and had some of these raised not only to remove obstacles in the harbour approaches but also for possible use in the proposed harbour works. Further, the disintegration of the north pier had allowed the sea to break through the loose stone barrier placed between McCook's Craig and the westerly end of the mail berth thus allowing the Craig to revert to its original condition of a detached rock.

During the winter of 1858 and the following spring, Vetch arranged for the removal of most of Smeaton's pier. There had been a partial collapse in 1853 and the debris constituted a danger greater than the benefit being derived from the remaining structure. Vetch reconstructed about 38 feet of the pier to provide shelter for small boats and so keep them well out of the way of the mail packets once reinstated. He also had a pathway cut out of the rock round McCook's Craig so that help could more easily reach any vessel driven on to the Craig.

The remainder of the plan from the Harbour Department was approved by the Treasury but even here the Admiralty had to take a minimalist approach. A new basin of modest size was to be excavated

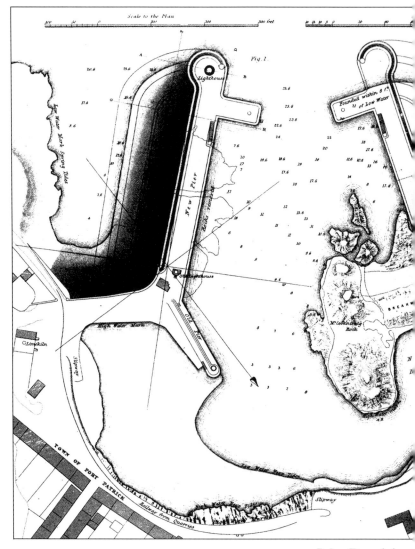

Scale to the Plan

Fig. 1

Lighthouse

Founded within 8 f.
of Low Water

New Pier

Old Lighthouse

Old Pier

Low Water Mark Spring Tides

High Water Mark

C. Limekiln

Slipway

McCockumeig Rock

BREAK

TOWN OF PORT PATRICK

Railway from Quarries

Slipway

John Rennie's p

34

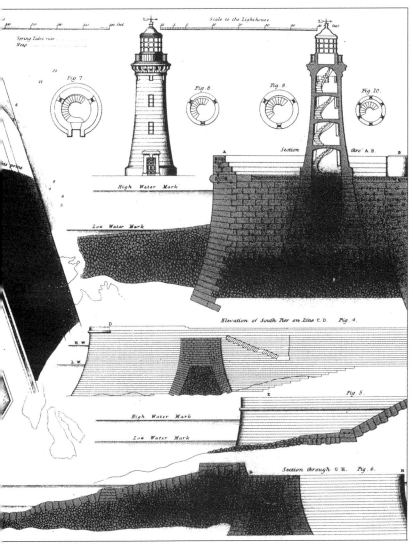

Spring Tides rise
Neap

Scale to the Lighthouse

Fig 7.

Fig. 8.

Fig 9.

Fig 10.

Section   thro' A.B.

High   Water   Mark

Low   Water   Mark

Elevation of South Pier on Line C.D.   Fig. 4.

H. W.

L. W.

Fig 5.

High   Water   Mark

Low   Water   Mark

Section through G.H.   Fig. 6.

Portpatrick Harbour.

35

to the north of the mail berth. A channel would connect it round the "elbow" presented by McCook's Craig to the harbour entrance. Some rock to the east of the old mail berth had to be removed. When designing the basin, the department had to provide as small a basin as was consistent with the employment of 150 feet-long steam packets. These steamers would require sufficient space in the basin to be turned — the weather exposure and physical shape of the harbour precluded the packets reversing in or out of Portpatrick. So, the principal berth on the east side of the rectangular basin was 287 feet long and the width of the basin was 202 feet. The entrance to the basin between two offset piers was some 80 feet. The area of the basin was $1\frac{1}{8}$ acres, an indication of its modest size.

It is difficult to know who was the greater culprit: the Treasury for refusing to accept the advice of experts as to the essential nature of the completion or some adaptation of the north pier, or the Admiralty for proceeding with the works in the full knowledge that everyone associated with the project knew that the lack of protection from the south-west through north-west would render the harbour unreliable and in constant need of repair.

In December 1858, James Abernethy, CE, was engaged by the Admiralty and sent to Portpatrick to prepare detailed plans. He was given the assistance of Captain Edward Hawes and Alexander Hannay, the Admiralty's foreman of works at Portpatrick. Abernethy was able to report to the Admiralty in February 1859 and gave an estimated cost of £19,400 with a construction period of twelve months. In his report, Abernethy indicated agreement with Vetch's assessment that the north pier should be extended. On the 15th July 1859, Parliament approved £20,000.

By October 1859 there appeared to be an impasse between the Admiralty and the Treasury. From the Admiralty: Vetch insists that the north pier be completed to provide a reliable harbour, but the Treasury refuses to go to parliament for the funds, "under these circumstances no further steps have been taken for commencing the works". From the Treasury: "can we be given an assurance that Abernethy's estimate is sufficient to do the job?"

The same month, October 1859, a rather nervous secretary of the Belfast & County Down Railway (B&CDR) informed the Treasury that the contract had been signed for the extension of the line from Newtownards to Donaghadee. Also, the company had invested in the railway being built to Portpatrick. His directors respectfully enquired when work would begin at Portpatrick.

There was also anxiety on the part of the Portpatrick Railway (PR) directors who, late in 1859, had still not contracted for the con-

Portpatrick Harbour from the North Cliff, c.1880. The south pier with its jetty is clearly seen. The lighthouse at the seaward end has been dismantled. Above the landward end of the south pier can be seen the quarry which supplied much of the stone for the harbour.

Photo: By courtesy of Allan A. Rankin.

struction of the difficult seven miles of track between Stranraer and Portpatrick. The Treasury stated firmly that no work would be done at Portpatrick Harbour until the railway company entered into the contract. To no avail did the railway argue that a sufficient guarantee of performance had been given by the railway company in the form of the stipulation in the parliamentary act authorising the company that no dividend could be paid until the line was completed to Portpatrick Harbour. The railway blinked first and a contract was signed in January 1860 for the line's construction. In early March 1860, the Galloway Advertiser reported the arrival at Portpatrick of two schooners with "engines, wagons, barrows, etc." for the railway works. Work on the line was to start immediately.

By contrast, there was no sign of any work on the harbour and it must have been galling for the railway company to receive a letter in April 1860 from the Admiralty admonishing "it is important that no further time be wasted". The occasion of the letter was the transfer of the land required for the basin (The railway was authorised by its act of parliament to acquire the land). Correspondence now went back and forward with plans shaded in light blue, dark blue, and red. The matter was finally settled in November.

But in March 1861, the PR wrote asking when work at the harbour was to start. The next delay was when the Admiralty realised that the harbour branch of the railway would pass through the Admiralty yard on the north side of the projected basin (Would this not have been obvious to the Harbour Department when preliminary plans were being drawn up, or was the original intention that the railway come along the east side of the basin?) The Admiralty demanded compensation and the matter dragged on for years. By the time the issue was settled (five years later!) responsibility for Portpatrick Harbour had been transferred (in 1863) from the Admiralty to the Board of Trade.

It would appear that work on the Portpatrick Harbour improvements started in the spring of 1861 when an act was passed allowing the Admiralty to close the harbour. The Downpatrick Herald reported the inspection of the new line to Donaghadee. To celebrate the occasion the tug/steamer Wonder was chartered by the B&CDR on Thursday, 23rd, May 1861, to take the Board of Trade inspector and railway officials over to inspect the work at Portpatrick. The weather was nasty with a strong north-west wind and rain squalls, but the Wonder completed the trip in three minutes over two hours. No indication is given in the report of the reaction of the railway officials to what they saw but the Herald correspondent closed with the statement that "several months must elapse before Portpatrick harbour is ready to receive vessels of a proper size". The officials would not find much to lift their

Another view of Portpatrick Harbour from the North Cliff. The remains of the harbour station can be seen in the lower left-hand corner.

Photo: By courtesy of Allan A. Rankin.

The Portpatrick Lighthouse recreated in Colombo, Sri Lanka.

Photo: 1999, Courtesy of David Williamson.

spirits that day and as the *Wonder* punched her way home into the headwind they must have wondered (pun intended) on the implications of what they had seen — or not seen — for the future of their new line to Donaghadee.

By February 1862, the excavation of the new basin was reported as "nearly complete" but it was July 1863 before the basin was flooded. On Saturday, 25th July, 1863, a large crowd had travelled by rail to Portpatrick — the railway from Stranraer had been open for almost a year — to observe the spectacle, but discovered that for once the work was completed ahead of schedule and the sea had been admitted the previous day.

Abernethy now started on clearing the debris and silt in the main channel from the harbour entrance, round the elbow of McCook's Craig and into the new miniature basin. In mid-August, the steam dredger from Ayr was brought by a tug to the harbour and remained until the end of November.

A single volume of copy letters from Alexander Hannay, the foreman at Portpatrick, to James Abernethy has survived and is now in the Stranraer Museum. The letters, spanning November 1863 to February 1865, give some sense of the challenges presented by the work. On the 4th February 1864, Hannay informed Abernethy that, once again, the breakwater linking McCook's Craig with the north pier had been partially washed away during one of the winter's gales. In late May, Hannay indicated that he hoped to have the basin ready to receive steamers in about six weeks. Work on the channel was continuing. He had three diving bells in use: one at the basin entrance and two in the outer harbour. In addition, a "helmet diver is constantly employed". A measure of the scale of operations is reflected in the reduction of the workforce from 170 to 110 once the winter approached.

The railway had reached Portpatrick in August 1862 and material now came down to the harbour by the short but steep branch from the town station. The Dinvin Burn which ran through the Admiralty yard under the cliff face was placed in a culvert and the station area — if the basic single platform can be so described — was laid out between the north side of the basin and the cliff face. In a letter of the 11th April, 1864, Hannay reported to Abernethy that £11.4.8d (£11.23p) was owed to the PR for damage to wagons. The wagons had been bringing timber down the harbour branch when a combination of slippery rails and the poor braking power of the wagons meant that the "men lost command of them, and rushing down with tremendous velocity, they smashed themselves on the terminal parapet".

The seven miles between Stranraer and Portpatrick had some long steep gradients, but the harbour branch with a gradient of 1 in 35 must have been close to the limit for safety and operation.

But Abernethy had had enough and on the 12th December 1864 Hannay wrote to him, "For my own sake I am very sorry that you have declined to act any longer as Engineer, and more so, if I have contributed to cause you to come to that decision". James Abernethy, bruised and bloodied like many before him, retreated from the scene.

The challenge was now taken up by Captain Edward Hawes when the Admiralty placed him in charge of the works at Portpatrick.

Work at Portpatrick was finally abandoned in 1866 and thereafter little effort was made to arrest the continuing erosion of the harbour. But something was salvaged. After lying idle for thirty years, the lighthouse at the seaward end of the south pier was dismantled in 1869 and in 1871 was shipped out to Colombo, Sri Lanka, and rebuilt (The current lighthouse at Portpatrick was built in 1883).

3. STEAM COMES TO THE ROUTE

1825 saw a dramatic change on the crossing. First, on the last day of 1824, the Post Office was, once again, authorised to place its own vessels on all the Irish Sea mail routes (An exception was of Liverpool-Isle of Man which remained in private hands). Second, private operators had demonstrated the potential of a new technology, namely ships propelled by steam engines (As early as 1815 — only three years after the pioneering steamship *Comet* appeared on the Clyde — Portpatrick saw its first steamship when the paddler *Elizabeth* took shelter while on her way from the Clyde to the Mersey).

In 1823, the Marquis of Downshire, head of the Donaghadee Packet Company, had requested that the company be authorised to replace its sailing packets with steam vessels and had investigated the purchase or charter of a steamer. But the Post Office was to place its own steam packets on the route and so the Donaghadee Packet Company was given six-months' fees as compensation and the company's packet boats laid up. Word reached Portpatrick in January 1825 that two steam vessels were to be sent north in the spring for the mail crossing. No longer would folk be "waiting for a wind".

In May, the Dumfries Courier reported that "On Saturday last [30th April 1825] there arrived at Portpatrick from the Thames, HM steam packets the *Dasher*, Captain Smithett, and the *Arrow*, Captain Pascoe, to be employed in the conveyance of the mail betwixt that port and Donaghadee. Both these steam packets are newly and completely fitted out for the service, and afford the most elegant accommodation for passengers".

The newspaper, recognising that the new steam packets were only one link in the chain, continued "Nothing will be wanting to restore the Donaghadee-Portpatrick station to its former pre-eminence, excepting a safe coach road betwixt Glasgow and the latter place, the want of which is by no means creditable to the nation. The valuable correspondence betwixt the north of Ireland and the West of Scotland is entrusted to a boy on horseback, for it is impossible to put a four-horse coach on the present road without great danger. It is to be hoped that the gentlemen of Ayrshire will soon take the necessary steps for removing the stigma from their fine county of being destitute of a good turnpike road".

The House of Commons Select Committee which, in 1823, recommended the employment of steam packets on the Portpatrick crossing, also commented unfavourably on the state of the road linking Glasgow and Portpatrick (Almost two centuries later, the same complaints are being heard about the poor access to the south-west corner of Scotland provided by the A75 and A77).

By today's standards, *Dasher* and *Arrow* were small. Their wooden hulls were about 100 feet in length (For comparison, *Stena Caledonia* sailing between Stranraer and Ireland is just over 400 feet). But the sailing packets they replaced were only about 40 feet long and one observer described the two steamers as "so splendidly fitted up as to deserve the name of floating palaces". The steamships were 17 feet 3 inches in the beam and drew 6 feet of water. The successful use of the propeller as a means of propulsion still lay some years in the future and the ships were driven by paddles each powered by a side lever engine of 20 horse power. *Dasher* and *Arrow* had been built on the Thames in 1821 and were the pioneer steamships carrying the mail between Dover and Calais. Their speed is variously reported as 8 or 10 knots. The packets carried three masts and, as was common at the time, the boiler and so the funnel, were aft of the engines.

Captain E.R. Pascoe hailed from Milford Haven and Luke Smithett considered Dover as home. Neither was familiar with the idiosyncrasies of the harbours and the currents of the crossing, and the captains from two of the Donaghadee Company's packets, Hamilton Cranston of the *Hillsborough* and James McConnell of the *Palmer*, joined the ranks of the Post Office and were appointed "sailing masters" of the steamships. Their title reminds us that steam was then considered by many as complementing rather than replacing sail as a means of propulsion. *Dasher* and *Arrow* each had an engineer and a fireman as well as a mate and three or four seamen. The ships' complements were completed with a steward who would attend to travellers' needs in the saloon aft — we are told that breakfast was available. Modest shore establishments were set up at both Portpatrick and Donaghadee with, primarily, boatmen who helped the paddlers negotiate the harbours and also attended to loading coal. A carpenter was in place at Portpatrick for minor repairs but for major work and overhauls the ships had to go to the government's dockyard at Holyhead. The trips south were once a year for each of the packets (Later, a storekeeper was appointed to take charge of the coal yard at Portpatrick).

The steam packets entered service almost immediately and the Belfast Newsletter of the 6th May 1825 reported: "Donaghadee —May 4. 9.00 a.m. arrived HM steam packet *Dasher*, Captain Smithett, with the mail from Portpatrick after a passage of $2^{1}/_{2}$ hours. The *Dasher* is a remarkably fine vessel. 1 p.m. sailed HM packet *Dasher*, with the mail and passengers".

The following day, the arrival of *Arrow* at 9 a.m. after a crossing of 2 hours 25 minutes was reported. This reflected the pattern that evolved of using the packets on approximately alternate days. In those far-off days, steam engines and boilers were "high maintenance" items and a "day off" between sailings was a wise move. Even then, the mail would still be conveyed from time to time by sailing packet especially when one of the steam packets was at Holyhead for refit, thus leaving the other steamer alone on the crossing.

The service soon settled down to a pattern of the mail from London arriving at Portpatrick an hour or so before midnight while that from Glasgow was expected around 5 a.m. The packet would sail at 6 a.m. for Donaghadee, returning from the Irish side around mid-day. The mail took about two and a half hours to travel between Donaghadee and Belfast.

Apart from a serious interruption in the first year (see below), the reliability was dramatically improved. Surviving records for the 1820s show that the Donaghadee sailing packets failed to cross almost every fourth day. By contrast, the steam packets would miss only 12 or 15 days a year (Sometimes the crossing was abandoned because of a break in the land link on account of floods or snow). Also, it was now quite common for the new ships to make the crossing in less than three hours — a very rare occurrence with the sailing packets. There were still some very long passages. The mail that left Donaghadee at 12.25 p.m. on the16th January, 1828, did not reach the Scottish shore until the following morning at 10.40 when landfall was made at Port Mullen at the north end of the Rhinns of Galloway. There were other occasions when weather forced the packets to shelter in Loch Ryan and the mail was landed at Cairnryan or Stranraer.

The timetable for the 95-mile Glasgow-Portpatrick mail gives us a sense of the speed of travel — in 1832, in this case.

Glasgow, leave	4.45 p.m.
Kilmarnock, arrive	7.30
Ayr, arrive	9.00
Girvan, arrive	11.38
Ballantrae, arrive	1.16 a.m.
Portpatrick, arrive	5.06

We should not be misled by the precision. This timetable was an example of the victory of hope over experience! Above, mention was made of the dissatisfaction with the land connections to Portpatrick from both Dumfries and Glasgow. The Post Office calculated that the average speed from Dumfries to Portpatrick was 7.6 m.p.h. while that from Glasgow was 7.7 m.p.h. This contrasted with the average speed for the London mails which between the capital and Dumfries managed an average of 9.6 m.p.h.

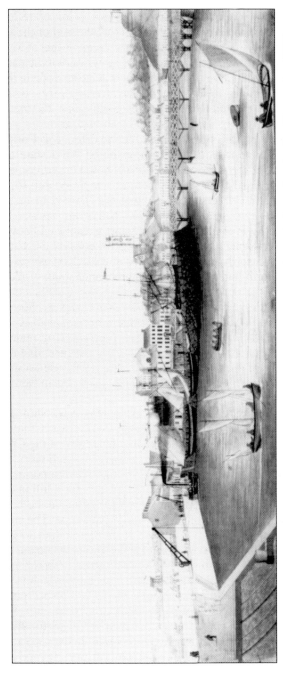

View of Donaghadee Harbour from the South Quay. Pen and wash drawing by D. Kennedy, 1832.

Copyright – Ulster Folk and Transport Museum, Northern Ireland (Neg. L5071).

When *Dasher* and *Arrow* arrived in the spring of 1825, work on Donaghadee Harbour was well along and by the end of the year the entire south pier was available with depths of up to 18 feet at low water spring tides. The accompanying illustration shows one of the packets in the harbour. We notice some paving work is still being done in the foreground on the south pier. Also of interest is the temporary wooden pier in the right background, linking the north pier to the shore. Delacherois' harbour is in the centre of the picture.

A similar happy story cannot be reported for Portpatrick. Despite newspaper reports of the harbour being "in a state of great forwardness," there were serious impediments to be overcome by the packets. Neither the north or south pier was completed and so, to provide a berth for the packets, John Rennie was forced to resort to a makeshift arrangement. At high tide, McCook's Craig was an island. A rubble breakwater with some masonry support was placed between the Craig and the north pier. The area contained between the Craig, the breakwater, and the north pier was quarried and dredged as was a channel linking the "north harbour" to the main channel south of the Craig. The north harbour now provided for the packets a berth, albeit cramped, with 8 feet of water at low tide. Nature worked away at returning the area to the way it had been before. The breakwater was subject to constant erosion — not helped by the habit of people taking material off the shore around the breakwater (It appears, for example, that much of the rubble infill used in the construction of the lighthouse on the south pier came from the breakwater). Also, the channel and basin were always filling up with silt and stones.

A glance at the map of Portpatrick Harbour will show that the packets when leaving the mail berth inside McCook's Craig had to make a 180° turn in a confined space round the elbow of the Craig and then set a course between the unfinished north and south piers. If there was wind of any weight from the south through west to north, a lookout was placed on the north pier who would watch for a lull in the seas rolling in. On word being given, the packet would leave the berth and swing round the end of McCook's Craig on a heavy rope. The engineers would then extract the maximum power from the engines to give the bucking packet some steerage way as it headed out between the piers. A similar heart-stopping procedure had to be followed when entering the harbour. A buoy would be plucked out of the water by a seaman on the packet as it lurched into the harbour between the unfinished piers. The buoy was attached to a length of rope which in turn was attached to a check cable. The other end of the cable was attached to McCook's Craig. The crew on the packet would quickly pull up the rope and wrap the cable round a bollard and so take the way off the ship and allow it to spin round into the mail berth.

What is meant to help can sometimes prove to be a hindrance. When Captain Pascoe was taking *Dasher* out one morning in October 1825 the starboard paddle ran over the buoy lying just off McCook's Craig. The buoy, the rope, and the cable wrapped themselves around the paddle wheel before it could be stopped. The paddle was immobilised and the strong south-west wind pushed *Dasher* on to the Craig where, it seemed at first, she would be smashed into pieces by the heavy seas. But the bravery and skill of the boatmen who immediately set off from the shore resulted in the packet being pulled clear of the Craig and she landed on the sandy shore. Massive damage was done to the hull, and starboard engine and paddle wheel. The passengers did not escape unscathed. One poor woman was subjected to the amputation of a leg which had been crushed between the hull and the rock. She did not survive the surgery. As the newspaper reported, "Many of the passengers lost bundles, hats, etc. but they seemed very content that they escaped with their lives".

Dasher was taken off to the dockyard at Holyhead and it was mid-March of 1826 before she returned to the route. Captain Smithett was despatched to Glasgow in an unsuccessful search for a suitable ship to be chartered to cover for *Dasher*. In the interim, the mail was carried on several days by sailing ships which were already trading between Portpatrick and Donaghadee.

Dasher survived this time, but she was not so fortunate on Sunday, 19th December, 1830. She left Portpatrick, late, at 7.30 a.m. and, punching into heavy seas, she did not appear off Donaghadee until 4.30 p.m. The seas running prevented *Dasher* from entering the harbour and a boat was sent out for the exchange of mail. The passengers were forced to remain on board for the return crossing to Portpatrick. A boiler explosion put the engines out of action and the sails were set. With the wind behind her, *Dasher* made good time and she was off Portpatrick by 7.00 p.m. As she approached the harbour a combination of broken seas, current and a sudden squall rendered her temporarily unmanageable. It took only a few seconds of these conditions to cause *Dasher* to miss the entrance and she was driven heavily on to rocks two hundred yards south of the harbour. *Dasher* quickly began to break up and the passengers and crew scrambled ashore. Again, a woman passenger succumbed to injuries received. The strength of the storm was such that the mailbag and bits of *Dasher* were found on the shore of the Isle of Man two weeks later.

The difficulties experienced leaving and entering the harbour were aggravated by the constant build-up of sand and rubble in the area of the mail berth. Smeaton's pier deftly deflected the force of the sea into that corner of the harbour but it could not be removed since it provided the only shelter for the sailing ships still using the harbour. We have reports of a dredging machine being brought to Portpatrick to clear away the build-up off the mail berth. The presence of the dredger, of course, presented yet another navigational obstacle for the packets and sometimes while the dredger was in the harbour the packets would have to resort to Loch Ryan in bad weather. But the benefits from dredging did not seem to last beyond the next real storm. If the packet's scheduled departure in the morning fell near low tide, the packet would leave early and lie off the harbour, per-haps for two hours or more, awaiting the boat bringing out the mail and passengers. Today, this part of the harbour is still a shallow "bar" off the entrance to the new inner basin.

A replacement for *Dasher* was sent north. *Fury* had been built in 1824 for the Dover mail station and was very similar to her prede-cessor at Portpatrick. In 1833, *Arrow* returned to Dover where private vessels were increasingly attracting passengers away from the mail packets. *Arrow* was lengthened and outfitted with new paddle wheels, boiler and engines. To take the place of *Arrow* at Portpatrick, *Spitfire*, sister of *Fury*, came north.

Fury and *Spitfire* were six feet shorter than the vessels they replaced. This feature would probably make them marginally easier to handle within the confines of Portpatrick Harbour. The mail packets were still using the "temporary" berth between McCook's Craig and the north pier. The south pier was completed in 1833 but without the north pier there was no protection for vessels lying alongside the south pier berth.

It was generally conceded that the mail packets were under-powered for the conditions they encountered on the short sea crossing. In 1832, *Fury* was taken in hand at the Holyhead dockyard and a new boiler and wheels were fitted, and in 1833 new, larger cylinders fitted, increasing the horsepower of each of her engines to 25. In 1834, it was the turn of *Spitfire* to be similarly upgraded. Even so, we must assume that the vessels were pushed to their limits on many crossings.

While the primary concern of the Post Office was the transporta-tion of the mails, the packet boats carried a fair number of passengers. In fact, an oddity of the Treasury's accounting procedures when striking a profit or loss for the various routes was to limit the revenue to that earned from carrying passengers. No attempt was made to credit the routes with any portion of postage earned. Likewise, the greatly improved reliability and increasing volume of mail were ignored. On this basis, the Portpatrick route, like the other Irish Sea routes, appeared to be operating at a loss. Two years of financial results for the Portpatrick station were presented to a parliamentary committee in 1832 and reflect this. Table 2 shows the numbers and comparison figures are given for other Irish Sea routes which show Portpatrick was not the financial drain that others were.

Table 2: Financial Results for Portpatrick and Other Stations, 1830, 1831.

	1830	1831
Packet agent (1)	£300	£300
Captains (2)	500	500
Wages of seamen (12)	795	811
Engineers (4)	218	218
Coals	637	603
Repairs to vessel and supplies	446	476
Repairs to engines	96	30
Rent	5	9
Incidentals	84	246
	£3081	£3193
Receipts from passengers, etc	2126	2114
Excess costs for year	£(955)	£(1078)
Holyhead station, excess costs	£(12,042)	£(13,806)
Liverpool station, excess costs	£(2359)	£(9126)
Milford station, excess costs	£(9534)	£(10,171)

Source: Parliamentary Papers 1831-32 (716), XVII, p326.

Naturally, with this method of accounting, the Post Office was inclined to push passenger charges as high as the market would bear and this provoked constant criticism. After yet another roasting by a government committee, the Post Office reduced its rates. For the record, the fares applying on the Portpatrick-Donaghadee crossing are shown in Table 3.

Table 3: Rates applying on Portpatrick route in 1825 and 1837.

	1825-March 1837	April 1837—
Cabin passengers	8/- (40p)	5/- (25p)
Children, under 10yrs	5/- (25p)	2/6d (12$\frac{1}{2}$p)
Servants & cattle drovers	5/- (25p)	3/- (15p)
Harvestmen & paupers	2/- (10p)	—
Deck passengers	—	1/6d (7 $\frac{1}{2}$p)
Four-wheeled carriages	£2 (£2)	£1.5/- (£1.25p)
Two-wheeled carriages	15/- (75p)	12/6d (62$\frac{1}{2}$p)
Horses	8/- (40p)	5/- (25p)
Rent of after cabin, not exceeding six persons	£3 (£3)	£3 (£3)

Sources: Parliamentary papers 1831-32 (716), XVII, p381
Parliamentary papers 1837-38 (203), XLV

The fare reduction was made in 1837, but criticism had been running high in 1832 when a price war was waging between two companies running directly between Glasgow, Greenock and Belfast. G. & J. Burns were offering a cabin fare of 2/6d (12$\frac{1}{2}$p). But at that time, the Post Office fought off the attempts to have it lower its charges. It did, however, accept the recommendation from a government committee that a two-tier fare structure be introduced for deck passengers (i.e. passengers not claiming access to the cabin aft) with fares at 5/- and 2/-. At first, the sole criterion between the two fares was to be "the appearance of the individual"! Soon, the more workable category of "harvestmen and paupers" was adopted for the 2/- fare, as shown above. The committee's other recommendation that a 6d. (2$\frac{1}{2}$p) charge be introduced for dogs was ignored.

While the records do not directly reflect this, livestock was carried. A committee in 1836 was told that "cattle are carried causing offence to passengers". The same committee heard from Captain Henry of *Fury* on the difficulties posed by the "appearance of the individual" criterion. On one occasion, he related to the committee, he had been concerned that some families travelling were being annoyed by a group of drunken pig drivers who were insisting on being given access to the cabin. He had forbade them the use of the cabin and they had complained to the authorities in London. As a result, Captain Henry had been reprimanded and fined the difference between the 2/- and the 5/- fare for each of the pig drivers since the Post Office had been deprived of the revenue. The record is silent as to what the committee made of this episode.

The greater number of the passengers were in fact "deck", paying the 2/- fare. Each year in the 1825-1831 period, the packets carried about 12,000 passengers of which about 1,000 were typically "cabin" at 8/-. Also, the deck traffic was concentrated in August and September, reflecting the flows of temporary farm labour. It is remarkable to note that these small vessels carried carriages on the exposed crossing, usually around seventy each year. In some years, over 200 horses made the journey with their owners. Table 4 shows the carryings in the year to October 1828 and the seasonal pattern is clearly seen.

To allow some comparison with the fares, in the mid-1830s the boatmen at Portpatrick and Donaghadee were paid about 13/- (65p) per week and the commander of a mail packet received about £5 per week.

The passing of the Reform Act in 1832 was a sign of changing attitudes in the nation and at Westminster. Government departments came under increased scrutiny — the word we would use today is "accountability". The Post Office was an easy target and in 1835 a commission was appointed to "inquire into the management of the Post Office Department". The findings on the packet services were contained in the commission's Sixth Report, issued in 1836.

Table 4: Monthly figures for traffic between Portpatrick and Donaghadee, 11/1827 – 10/1828

	Passengers	Carriages	Horses
Nov 1827	962	1	19
Dec	768		7
Jan 1828	678	2	13
Feb	668	1	19
Mar	831	1	13
Apr	935	10	13
May	1013	4	12
Jun	989	5	23
Jul	1207	3	21
Aug	1571	18	26
Sep	1736	11	23
Oct	1259	8	43

Source: Parliamentary Papers 1830 (647). XIV, p494

It was recommended that the mail route be transferred to Larne in County Antrim on the Irish side and to a calling place in Loch Ryan on the Scottish side. At Larne a pier had been constructed which was sheltered and accessible at all states of the tide. The Antrim port now had steamboat links with Glasgow, Campbeltown, Oban, and Liverpool and the pier's owner had offered access to the mail packets at no charge.

The call for a change of route was ignored but another recommendation was acted upon. From the 16th January 1837, responsibility for the management of the Irish Sea, Channel Islands, English Channel mail routes was transferred from the Post Office to the Admiralty. The latter body had been operating the long-haul mail ships from Falmouth for some years. Sir Edward Parry was appointed Comptroller of Steam Machinery and Packet Services. We are told in his biography, Parry of the Arctic, that the "and Packet Services" was added almost as an afterthought but he found this area of his work to be a continual trial. As early as the spring of 1837, Parry had formed a negative opinion of Portpatrick. He wrote, "Upon the whole, I could scarcely have imagined a more wretched harbour for packets if I had not seen Portpatrick".

The Post Office continued to control the timings of the sailings. The only obvious change was that someone did not like the packets' names: at Portpatrick *Fury* became *Asp* and *Spitfire* became *Pike*. The Portpatrick Harbour Commissioners continued in their attempts at completing the harbour. No attempt was made by the Admiralty to make the plans more realistic in light of a dozen years of experience with the steam packets.

An issue which resurfaced in the 1836 report which will take on an increased importance later in our story was that of returning the conveyance of the mails to private operators. One route, Liverpool-Dublin was half-handed over to a private company, the City of Dublin Steam Packet Company, with effect from the 20th June, 1839. "Half-handed" since the company gave the evening sailing while the Admiralty gave a morning sailing. Since the bulk of passengers travelled with the evening sailing, the Admiralty lost out financially. But the principle of contracting with private operators was now back on the table and if any lessons were learned (and it is not clear if the Admiralty or the Post Office ever learned anything on operating steam packets!) it was that splitting between private and government operators did not work — not the least because the private firms were better negotiators.

Table 5: Passenger carryings on the Portpatrick route, 1825-1838.

	To Donaghadee		To Portpatrick	
	Cabin	Steerage	Cabin	Steerage
1825	569	6152	595	3481
1826	556	6580	557	5385
1827	447	6961	450	5178
1828	536	6712	539	4903
1829	459	6570	483	4868
1830	522	7069	554	5871
1831	520	6686	500	5942
1832	554	5399	430	3849
1833	427	4348	435	3847
1834	470	5171	483	4593
1835	429	4525	397	4249
1836	543	3566	519	4059
1837	531	3443	455	4103
1838 to 1/8	222	1670	213	2683

Sources: 1825-1831 Parliamentary Papers 1831-32 (716), XVII, p373
1832-1838 The New Statistical Account of Scotland, volume IV, p154

An Admiralty letter book for the Portpatrick station has survived. The period covered is the 1st January 1844 to the 12th June 1848 and the book is now part of the Stranraer Museum's collection. The copies of letters going to London are mostly daily reports on the station's activities and remind us that work at the station was humdrum with the occasional bursts of danger or excitement.

A typical report, taken from the 1st February 1844, reads: "Sir [Secretary of the Admiralty, London], I beg &c. that HMP *Asp* proceeded at 6.40 a.m. to Donaghadee with the London and Glasgow mails and returned at 2.20 p.m. with the Irish Mails of this date. The other duties, viz. *Pike's* crew airing sails, cleaning decks, overhauling rigging and spars. Engineers and firemen examining the Engines, shore department examining the moorings. Smith making new hinges for paddle box covers. Carpenter completing trifling defects to paddle box. *Asp's* crew completing coaling, cleaning up after the voyage, Engineers and firemen cleaning machinery. At 6 p.m. both packets coaled and ready for sea. *Asp* for tomorrow's mail" .

The letter book on the 22nd May 1844 reflects the receipt of "a commission for Commander Edward Hawes . . . appointing him additional commander of Her Majesty's Yacht the *Royal Sovereign* for the Packet Service at Portpatrick". Two months previous, commissions had been received for Lieutenants Alex. Boyter and William Oke likewise attached to the *Royal Sovereign*. This was the standard appointment procedure followed by the Admiralty (The writer is not a Royal Navy expert and is unclear as to the reason for the double appointment, unless it was because Portpatrick was not a regular establishment).

Hawes' connection at Portpatrick was to be a long one and would outlast the steam packets by over two decades. Early in 1847, Hawes received a request from the Earl of Auckland, First Lord of the Admiralty, for a confidential report on the situation at Portpatrick. Auckland's interest in 1847 may be traced to the impending transfer of responsibility for the harbour from the Portpatrick Harbour Commissioners to the Admiralty.

Twenty years later, when recollecting his 1847 report, Hawes displays a philosophical frame of mind.

"In entering on the subject, I was struck by the various and conflicting opinion, even of the most talented men, on the point. It was clear that the engineer and others, regarding only the short sea distance to Donaghadee, and the favourable position and power to make a quick passage, declared in its favour, while the scientific and experienced naval officer, regarding more forcibly its exposed position and the heavy sea at the entrance, decided against it".

On the 26th June 1847, Captain Hawes was informed that the Commissioners would be handing over responsibility for the harbour to the Admiralty. Hawes was invited to take charge of the harbour as well as continue as a commander of one of the packets — without additional salary, he would later point out. He adds: "Knowing how much annoyance and many difficulties we had to contend with in carrying on the mail service from the state of the harbour, I willingly consented, with the hope of removing these impediments".

The transfer of responsibility took place in September 1847. Hawes commented, "The state of the harbour at the time of this transfer to the Admiralty was not satisfactory". He lists the problems: a coffer dam used in the construction of the south pier had been only partially removed, leaving an obstruction covered by only three feet of water at low tide; the buildup of rubble, gravel and sand in the passage round McCook's Craig to the north harbour had reduced the depth at low tide to only three feet; the berth in the north harbour was just too small; water was deflected off Smeaton's pier onto a newly-erected cattle slip which bounced the sea directly into the mail berth, dictating heavy moorings to hold the packets; construction of the north pier had been abandoned in 1839 when the money had to be diverted to patch up the south pier, with the result that the north pier was now breaking up and not only collapsing into the main harbour channel but accelerating the rate of erosion of the breakwater from McCook's Craig and so increasing the exposure of the mail berth and the shore line to the full force of storms; finally, funding for the repair work on the south pier was so inadequate that the battle with nature was being lost.

Captain Hawes set to work. By 1849, the channel round the Craig was dredged — yet again — and the low tide depth improved to 6 feet 6 inches; the cattle slip removed which reduced the bound into the mail basin; the breakwater sheltering the mail berth was moved seventy feet westwards and the breakwater rebuilt. Hawes also managed to arrest the breaking up of the north pier by building up masonry at its truncated end. Looking back, he concluded, "The comparative tranquillity which even these few alterations gave, was satisfactory".

The scene we see today at the north-west corner inside McCook's Craig is very similar to what travellers on *Asp* and *Pike* would see in 1849, except a more permanent breakwater was erected in 1991 to arrest the erosion of the rubble breakwater. Actually, the breakwater had been broken and patched up several times before 1991.

Further, Captain Hawes also met a request from Auckland to submit plans for new steam packets for the Portpatrick station and he had been expecting to take delivery in 1850 of two new packets of "great power and capacity". But, he comments, "At this juncture Lord Auckland died, a change took place in the Admiralty, and a desire, which I believe, had before existed, to transfer the mails to Glasgow was carried out".

While Captain Hawes was much exercised over the physical condition of the harbour at Portpatrick, his concern also extended to the wellbeing of his staff. The parish minister later recalled an occasion when this concern almost got Hawes into trouble. One of the steam packets was approaching Portpatrick in heavy weather and although its commander wanted to attempt an approach, Hawes signalled him away to Loch Ryan. The minister recollected that the wives of the seamen on the packet were so incensed at this excessive caution that they were on the point of attacking him until cooler minds prevailed.

As Captain Edward Hawes concludes his reflection on his days with the steam packets, one can almost hear a sigh of frustration, "Throughout the whole history of this place, an uncertainty has attended it".

By the mid-1840s, the Treasury was pressing both the Admiralty and the Post Office to enter into contracts with private operators on the various mail routes. The Treasury saw an opportunity to save money while Auckland at the Admiralty argued that the service provided by the steam packets was more reliable and efficient than could be expected of a private operator. There was also the fear that if a private operator took over a route and the Admiralty dispersed its staff and disposed of its packets, the Post Office could find itself being blackmailed by the new incumbent carrier of the mail.

An act had been passed in 1815 which, in principle, accepted that private operators had a role to play in carrying the mails on the Irish Sea. The act required that the master of a ship receiving a mail bag would pay a deposit of 3/- (15p) to the post office agent. The deposit was returned on the delivery of the mail bag. The shipowner received 2d (0.8p) per letter carried. The legislation was an attempt to regulate what was already happening and customs officers were authorised to search ships for letters being carried irregularly.

In 1848, the rail link between London and Holyhead was completed and all mail from the capital to Ireland was now routed through Holyhead and Dublin. But the death blow to the Portpatrick crossing came when a shipowner offered to carry the mails between Scotland and Ireland free of charge.

The Glasgow shipowner, George Burns of G. & J. Burns, had heard in 1848 that the Post Office, bowing to the inevitable, was considering offering the mail contract to the Ardrossan Steam Navigation Company. This company operated a steamship service between Ardrossan and Belfast. There was a rail link between Ardrossan and Glasgow and the Ardrossan route to Ireland was in fierce competition with Burns' route to Belfast from the Broomielaw in Glasgow and Greenock.

While the Post Master General, Lord Clanricarde, might have been disposed to give the mail contract to Lord Eglinton's Ardrossan company, Burns' offer could not be brushed aside. After the Post

Office's experience with the City of Dublin company the offer to carry the mails free of charge was initially dismissed as the work of a crackpot, but Burns persisted.

February 1849

Sir [Secretary to the Post Office],

I beg to say that I am prepared to offer, and do hereby make offer, to convey free of all charge Her Majesty's Mails and Bags of Letters between Greenock and Belfast by steam vessels to sail from each port on the evening of each day (Sunday excepted), at such hours as shall be fixed by the Post Master General. The service to commence on Monday 2 July next, and be carried regularly by us, until terminated by either party giving three months' notice of their desire to end the agreement.

I have, etc.
George Burns

On the 21st February the Post Office sent a copy of Burns' offer to the Admiralty, urging the Admiralty to go along with the offer. The Post Office expected to save about £2,800 annually by transferring the mail to Burns' company. Never a department to rush things, it was two months before the Admiralty sent its reply in the affirmative.

On the last day of May, the Post Office wrote to Burns, accepting his offer. The Post Office asked for the service to include Sunday sailings as applied at Portpatrick. But Burns was a staunch sabbatarian and declined. He desperately wanted to deprive the Ardrossan Company of the cachet attaching to being the carrier of HM Mail, but would not compromise.

The change-over to Greenock and Belfast happened quickly and on the evening of Monday 9th July the mail travelled by train from Glasgow to Greenock where the newly-acquired paddle steamer *Camilla* awaited to carry the mail from Greenock to Belfast. To ensure reliability, Burns dedicated three paddlers to the route: *Lyra* and *Thetis* in addition to *Camilla*. Extensive improvements were carried out in Belfast Harbour in the 1840s and the opening of the second section of the Victoria Channel at Belfast in 1848 and extensive dredging in 1849 meant Belfast could be approached at any state of the tide by ships drawing up to 10 feet. Thus, as at Portpatrick, a fixed time schedule could be operated between Ireland and Scotland.

Vague promises came from London that Portpatrick would be kept ready to take over again should the need arise. No doubt some expected the "free of charge" to last for only a few months before their worst fears of being held blackmail for a large charge would be realised.

Burns refused to countenance Sunday sailings and on Sunday, 23rd, July 1849, the mail was carried through Portpatrick for Donaghadee. This would appear to have been the last day for the steam packets and the Portpatrick station was closed down and Captain Edward Hawes appointed Harbour Master. By the end of September 1849, both *Pike* and *Asp* had left for Portsmouth. *Pike* then lay inactive at Devonport until 1862 when she became a tender to *HMS Royal Adelaide*. This lasted for four years. After being laid up again, *Pike* was broken up in June 1868. *Asp* was in service for several years as a survey ship on the Irish Sea, operating first out of Holyhead and then Milford. In March 1865, *Asp* moved to Devonport as tender to *HMS Saturn*, and four years later started a spell at Chatham where she was involved with the extension of the dockyard. This veteran was broken up in the early 1880s.

Acting on behalf of the Admiralty, Captain Hawes began selling off the stores and equipment at Portpatrick, but was allowed to keep one of the large boats for harbour work. This boat, manned by a volunteer crew, quickly came to the aid of the Burns' steamer *Orion* which foundered just off Portpatrick in the early hours of the 18th June 1850 while en route from Liverpool to Glasgow.

The new mail service represented a major improvement for communication between Glasgow and Belfast. Table 6 shows a comparison issued by the Post Office in February 1850. Mail was now in both cities in time for the morning's first deliveries.

Not everyone was happy, however.

Table 6: A comparison of Portpatrick and Greenock routes, February 1850.

Glasgow lve. 4.30 p.m. via Portpatrick, Belfast arr. 9.15 a.m. $16^3/_4$ hours
Glasgow lve. 6 p.m., via Greenock, Belfast arr. 5 a.m. $\underline{11}$

Time saved $5^3/_4$ hours

Belfast lve. 7.15 a.m., via Donaghadee, Glasgow arr. 2 a.m. $18^3/_4$ hours
Belfast lve. 7 p.m., via Greenock, Glasgow arr. 6.30 a.m. $\underline{11^1/_2}$

Time saved $7^1/_4$ hours

Source: Parliamentary Papers HL 1850 (37), XX, p475

4. RAILWAY TO THE RESCUE

"There surely never was such a case of stultification and absurdity as proposing to abolish Portpatrick harbour, just at a time when the country has paid for finishing and completing it. And for what great countervailing good? In order to exchange a short sea passage of 18 miles for one of at least 90! . . . The arrangement proposed is really a most preposterous one. . . . Greenock of all places! The very farthest off that could have been selected. Take Ardrossan, Troon, Ayr, Girvan, Ballantrae, Cairnryan, Stranraer — but Greenock is a monstrous choice on this side".

Thus thundered the Galloway Advertiser and Wigtownshire Free Press of the 1st June 1849, on the announcement that the mail link between Portpatrick and Donaghadee was to be replaced by a service between Greenock and Belfast.

Petitions were drawn up and sent to the Prime Minister, the Post Office, and the Treasury. On Saturday, 17th June, 1849, a deputation met with Lord John Russell, the Prime Minister, Sir Francis Baring, Chancellor of the Exchequer, and the Marquis of Clanricarde, Post Master General. The arguments for the shortest sea route being the best sea route were revisited. The vessels employed on the route were denigrated: "shandrydans" ("any rickety or old-fashioned vehicle" O.E.D.), "Lilliputian craft". The handling of the mail was decried, "If the utmost ingenuity had been applied to make the arrangements as bad as possible, they could scarce have been made worse than they were".

But this was a time when the railway had captured the Victorian imagination. At the June meeting, the Marquis of Londonderry argued that the ability of the railway "by annihilating distance by land" strongly supported the case for maintaining the shortest possible sea route (The marquis did wonder whether the improved link between south-west Scotland and Ireland could be a mixed blessing when he cryptically added that "There might be local evils incident to this interchange of population".

Captain John Dalrymple, the local M.P., referred to a proposal to extend the railway system to Portpatrick (Lines already reached Dumfries to the east and Ayr to the north). Lord Clanricarde, the Post Master General, then made a concession which put the future of Portpatrick, the village, its harbour, and its sea links back on the roller coaster. In response to Dalrymple's plea, Clanricarde said, "If the railways were carried forward there can be no doubt that the present stations will be maintained". The Prime Minister was more circumspect and simply concluded the meeting with the promise that the "question will be considered further".

The commercial centres of Belfast and Glasgow quickly adjusted to the greatly improved links for mail, passengers, and cargo provided by the Burns' steamship service between Glasgow, Greenock and Belfast. For their time, the vessels employed were commodious and speedy. Greenock had been connected to Glasgow by a railway since 1841 and it was now possible to complete the journey between Glasgow and Belfast in relative comfort on an overnight journey. But forces in Down and Wigtownshire persevered in their attempt to get the route through Portpatrick and Donaghadee reopened and so retrieve prestige and lost commercial activity and provide much-needed traffic for their proposed railways. Despite the obvious limitations existing at Portpatrick because of size and exposure to weather, memorialists in January 1856 could still claim that "By re-establishing a regular transit between [Portpatrick and Donaghadee], the last impediment to an unrestricted circulation of traffic between Great Britain and Ireland will be removed, the Channel itself almost annihilated, and the proximity of the two countries reduced to contact".

The railway was the new irresistible force at work. On the Irish side, parliamentary approval had been given for a railway to link Donaghadee with Newtownards (and so Belfast) and the memorialists requested a Public Works Loan of £100,000, "at reasonable terms", to expedite the construction. On the Scottish side railways had already reached Maybole to the north of Portpatrick and Dumfries to the east. The memorialists pointed out that the extension of the line south from Maybole was currently being surveyed while a company was being formed to carry the line west from Dumfries to Castle-Douglas from which a further line was proposed which would link Castle-Douglas and Portpatrick, and so give the Portpatrick traffic access to the main line at Dumfries.

So, the railway companies said they would build the rail connection if the Treasury would appropriate the funds for improving the harbours. The Treasury said the money could be found if the Admiralty determined that Portpatrick and Donaghadee were the most suitable for the mail service and the Post Office adopt the route as the mail passage between Scotland and Ireland. The Post Office said it would send the mails via Portpatrick and pay a reasonable fee if private enterprise provided the actual steamboat connection.

The Admiralty considered the conflicting reports it had commissioned (Difficulty in getting agreement on anything bedevilled the route. For example, two reports of a gale on Saturday, 23rd February, 1836: "The western wall of the harbour at Portpatrick was materially damaged by the gale . . . The sea made a complete breach through it".

Shipping Gazette, 25.3.36; "Not one stone of masonry was moved and the government steam packet rode out the gale in perfect safety". (London) Times, 26.3.36).

One report came from Captain George Evans, RN. "Portpatrick is not, nor ever can be made, a safe harbour, either to run to or depart from in westerly or south-westerly gales, without incurring a most enormous expense". Donaghadee, he pointed out, "has not the capacity for admitting that length of vessel which alone can ensure regularity and safety". Evans favoured Cairnryan and Larne. His first visit to Portpatrick, as a commissioner to a Post Office inquiry coincided with the 1836 gale mentioned above parenthetically. Significantly, the inquiry was established in response to a petition from the merchants of Glasgow who called for transferring the mail station away from Portpatrick.

On the other hand, Captain James Vetch of the Harbour Department of the Admiralty and hydrographer John Washington were more positive. "Portpatrick and Donaghadee . . . only require a comparatively small outlay to render them available for the purpose required". Vetch and Washington, like the Treasury, could not bring themselves to admit that the funds expended in the 1820s and 1830s had probably been a waste of public money and the best policy was to walk away from Portpatrick.

The Admiralty reported to the Treasury in July 1856 that "Portpatrick and Donaghadee are the most suitable harbours between which a short sea passage can be best established; and that their Lordships do not consider any further local investigation necessary".

On the 15th August 1856, the Treasury issued a "minute" agreeing to make funds available for improvements at Portpatrick and Donaghadee provided private enterprise supplied a steamer service and built the rail connections: Donaghadee with Belfast, Portpatrick with Glasgow and Dumfries. The Admiralty was to report to the Treasury on the estimated cost of the work required at the two harbours. The Treasury's agreement was based on the initial estimates provided by the Admiralty of £10,000 at Donaghadee and £15,000 at Portpatrick.

"All questions, all differences, all rivalries are now at an end", proclaimed the Galloway Advertiser on Thursday, 28th August, 1856. But the cracks were already beginning to appear. In the previous week's issue, the editor had chided those suggesting that harbours other than Portpatrick should still be considered — "we could end up with nothing". No doubt the rebuke was provoked, in part, by the arrival on board the steamer *Semaphore* at Cairnryan on the afternoon of the 11th August of the Belfast Harbour Commissioners together with "a large number of influential merchants and inhabitants of Belfast". They met with representatives of the projected railway: George Guthrie, convener of the Railway Committee and Alex Ingram, interim secretary. The party also met with Alex Langlands, the Stranraer agent for the Glasgow and Stranraer Steam Packet Company which operated several services for passengers and freight, including a service between Stranraer and Belfast of a frequency that varied between weekly and fortnightly. The gentlemen from Belfast wanted to know about the possibility of Cairnryan on Loch Ryan becoming the departure point for Belfast. The railway officials would not commit themselves concerning Cairnryan and emphasised that the railway had to be completed to Portpatrick before any other possibilities could be explored. But the harbour commissioners expressed satisfaction when assured that the railway would touch Loch Ryan at Stranraer. It is relevant to note that after some years of delay, work was starting on improving the berthing facilities at Stranraer, hitherto tidally-restricted, by extending the burgh (west) quay.

The limitations of Portpatrick were implicitly acknowledged when a letter from Edward Hawes, harbour master at Portpatrick, appeared two weeks later in the Advertiser. He advocated dividing the mails, passengers, light goods via Portpatrick, and heavy commercial traffic via Loch Ryan.

In October and November 1856, meetings were held in Belfast and several towns in Galloway and Wigtownshire to raise capital for the railway. The high hopes of the railway promoters were reflected in the initial title, 'The British and Irish Grand Junction Railway'. "A great national undertaking", cried the (Belfast) Northern Whig (6.11.56). The act authorising the railway received the royal assent on the 10th August 1857. By then the more prosaic title of the Portpatrick Railway was used. At the request of the Treasury, the act contained a clause prohibiting the payment of any dividend before the line was opened to the north pier at Portpatrick. The Treasury saw the clause as close as it could get to a guarantee of performance by the railway before any funds were released for the harbour works (But the stipulation that Portpatrick was to be linked with Glasgow to the north was quietly ignored and the Treasury had to admit later that events had overtaken it and it had been out-manoeuvred).

Events now began to run in a parallel, if fumbling, fashion in four locations: the PR, with its base in Stranraer, entered into contracts for the construction of the line; likewise the Belfast & County Down Railway began planning its line to Donaghadee; the Board of Public Works would soon start the work at Donaghadee harbour; and the Treasury prepared material to get parliamentary approval for the funds. Significantly, there was little action to be seen at Portpatrick Harbour.

At Portpatrick, topography demanded a station on high land on the edge of the town. A branch line to the harbour area would run back down steeply from a junction immediately beyond the town station. At Donaghadee, the railway would sweep round from the south to a station immediately by the harbour. A branch line for cargo and livestock ran from the east side of the station on to the south pier.

James Abernethy, CE, was appointed engineer to execute the plans at Portpatrick Harbour. The plans called for a channel of some 120 feet in width from the harbour entrance to a new basin of about $1\frac{1}{8}$ acres in extent. Abernethy, once he visited Portpatrick, indicated twelve months should suffice for the work. He also urged the Admiralty in February 1859 not to lose sight of the importance of completing the north pier if the harbour was to be accessible in all weathers.

The sorry saga of building the new basin at Portpatrick is related in the chapter on "Building the Harbours". Suffice to say here that it was the spring of 1861 before work began. In July 1863, the sea was admitted to the new basin and work then started on clearing the channel round McCook's Craig. It would appear to have been late 1864 before the basin was accessible. But completion continued to elude. Work was suspended for the 1864-65 winter, and then in 1866 the harbour works ceased.

By contrast the work at Donaghadee had gone smoothly. Some remedial work at the harbour was completed during 1858 and the B&CDR's link between Newtownards (on the line to Belfast) and Donaghadee opened on June 3rd 1861. The Glasgow & Stranraer S P Co's *Albion* had been chartered by the B&CDR on the 22nd July to demonstrate what the future would hold. The paddler left Donaghadee and crossed to Portpatrick and then on to Stranraer. It is reported that 500 passengers travelled by the new train service from Belfast for the day excursion. *Albion* presumably berthed alongside the south pier at Portpatrick. The paddler had a very full day. Rather than send *Albion* "light" from Stranraer to Donaghadee, the Steam Packet Company advertised a day excursion *from* Stranraer and Portpatrick to Donaghadee with a connection to Belfast by "the new railway". *Albion* left Stranraer at 0600 and Portpatrick at 0800. Thus, by the time *Albion* reached Stranraer around 2300 on the 22nd, she had made two round trips between Stranraer and Donaghadee and made four calls at Portpatrick. It must have been the fervent prayer of the B&CDR that this is what the future held, but the company's prospects were not sure.

The B&CDR had put all its eggs in the Donaghadee basket by building the railway to Donaghadee and investing in the PR: the line opened on the 3rd June 1861 and the investment was £15,000. On the other hand, the PR had options other than Portpatrick. The PR opened its line from Castle-Douglas to Stranraer on the 11th March 1861.

This provided a rail link through from a main north-south line at Dumfries. Ships of the Glasgow & Stranraer S P Co increased their Stranraer-Belfast frequency to twice weekly with the paddle steamers *Scotia* and *Albion*. It was now possible to leave London (Euston) at 2100 and reach Belfast at 1700 the next day via Stranraer. A similar return service was also available.

An obvious solution from the point of view of the PR was to abandon Portpatrick as the port for Ireland and get the Post Office to send the Irish mail through Stranraer to Belfast. Irish interests in Antrim had petitioned the Treasury as early as 1859 to abandon Portpatrick as hopeless and instead have the railway extended from Stranraer to Cairnryan on the north-east shore of Loch Ryan. It was claimed that if Larne were to be made a mail station with a steamboat connection from Cairnryan, the Belfast & Northern Counties Railway would be extended from Carrickfergus to Larne and so link the port with Belfast. The estimated passage time between Cairnryan and Larne was two hours. The Treasury replied that agreements had been entered into and the matter could not be re-opened. The PR had unsuccessfully approached the Treasury to allow a Stranraer-Larne route to be sub-stituted for the original route via Portpatrick. Even so, the promoters of the Carrickfergus & Larne Railway proceeded in 1860 and obtained parliamentary authorisation for the line in May.

The Carrickfergus and Larne Railway was effectively part of the Belfast and Northern Counties Railway and the B&NCR recognized an opportunity in the lack of progress at Portpatrick. The G. & J. Burns Belfast - Glasgow steamer *Giraffe* was chartered for a day in September 1860 and a "large and influential deputation" from the railway company made an 0800 hours departure from Belfast. *Giraffe* sailed round to the entrance of Donaghadee harbour and then made a $1^1/_4$ hour crossing to Portpatrick, again not berthing. The deputation continued on to Cairnryan where they met a deputation from the PR and argued that their observations that morning made Stranraer the only viable port for the crossing with, of course, Larne providing a good rail connection on to Belfast.

Initially, the intention at Stranraer had been to include a branch off the main line to Portpatrick. The branch was to run along the fore-shore to the Stranraer burgh (west) pier. In late 1860, the branch was realigned to run onto a new pier at Stranraer — the railway (or east) pier. Commencing on the 1st October 1862, the new steamer *Briton* operated a daily (except Sunday) round trip between Stranraer and Larne. This date coincided with the opening of the line linking Larne and Carrickfergus (and so Belfast). The branch line to the new east pier at Stranraer was not quite complete but it was placed in use anyway. *Briton* operated under the name of the Stranraer & Larne Steamboat Company. Since none of the railway companies involved had the authority to own and operate steamships, the ship was registered in the name of James McDowall of the PR and he was indemnified against losses by a consortium of railway companies with a financial interest in the success of the route.

The future was beginning to look a little better for the PR but the B&CDR was not at all happy. The day before *Briton* inaugurated the Larne route, a meeting of the PR shareholders was convened in Stranraer. A contingent of B&CDR shareholders crossed from Donaghadee to Portpatrick on the tug/steamer *Wonder* and proceeded to Stranraer for the meeting. The chairman of the PR tried to placate the Irish contingent by describing the Larne service as experimental and not intended as any more than a stopgap. The gentlemen were not convinced and their apprehensions must have increased when on arrival back at Portpatrick they learned that the wind had freshened to the extent that *Wonder* would not be able to make the return crossing that day. It was reported that some had to return to Stranraer and cross on *Briton's* inaugural trip to Larne.

The prospects for the Portpatrick route began slowly to unravel. By 1864, the Post Master General had lost interest. When a petition was received from Larne business interests arguing against a B&CDR proposal to allow a Stranraer-Donaghadee service, the PMG's response on the 8th July 1864 was revealing:

"As the whole matter, which is not one of much importance in a postal point of view, rests upon a promise made by the Treasury some years ago, I think it right to forward this application to [the Treasury]".

Separately, the Post Office had made it clear to the Treasury that all mails between England, Scotland and most of Ireland would be sent via Holyhead for the foreseeable future. The Holyhead route was "very costly" and could only be justified if nearly all mails used it. Mail from the Glasgow area would continue to go via Greenock since the carriage by Burns' steamers was still free. In the spring of 1865, the Post Office concluded that there was "little want of this additional communication by Portpatrick and Donaghadee".

In November 1865, the Treasury began to wash its hands of the whole affair by commenting that "the question has assumed a character not contemplated by the Treasury Minute of the 15th August 1856".

Responsibility for Portpatrick Harbour had by this time passed to the Board of Trade which made its views quite clear to the Treasury in November 1866,

"The Board of Trade trust they may no longer be the instru-

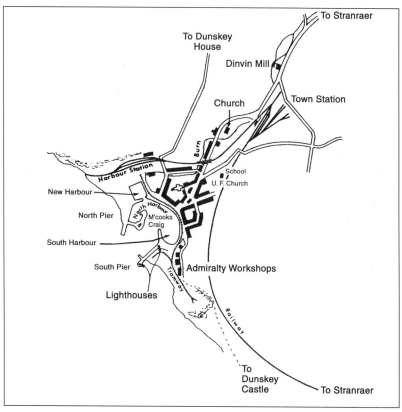

Portpatrick in 1865.

ments of wasting public money by carrying out an undertaking which was originally vicious, and which can never be, in their opinion, of any public service".

The government departments wanted out. The railway companies now positioned themselves to receive maximum compensation for the government's failure to deliver on the commitments made in the August 1856 Treasury Minute.

The PR commissioned a report from Luke Smithett, now Sir Luke, who had brought *Dasher* to the route some forty years before in 1825. Based on his investigating, Sir Luke gave a glowing report and concluded, "I consider nothing is more needed for carrying on the service in a satisfactory manner". Smithett argued for a double daily service and observed that the problems in the past had always been getting the steamships into the harbour but not out, so he saw no problem with having a night service provided the schedule called for the ships to leave Portpatrick in the late evening and return in the daylight. The Treasury was not convinced and the report was brusquely dismissed.

The PR wrote urging that the government not act precipitately and offered a daily special mail service between London and Belfast via Portpatrick at the annual cost of £14,690. The Treasury replied that this cost could not even be a beginning point of negotiation. The PR chairman expressed himself "utterly at a loss to express his surprise". The chairman was further appalled by the offer contained in the Treasury's letter to transfer responsibility and ownership of the incomplete harbour at Portpatrick over to the railway company. He argued that if the government now found Portpatrick unsuitable for the mail service, then the obvious solution was to send the mail via Stranraer.

The jousting continued as the Treasury now expressed surprise at the reluctance of the PR to accept ownership of Portpatrick harbour, especially since the Treasury thought it was "offering a property the merits of which had been much pressed upon them by the company".

The PR had now discovered that the B&CDR had in July 1867 worked out with the Treasury acceptable compensation for the abandonment of the route. The PR had assumed that this agreement had been made to open up the possibility of sending the mail via Stranraer to either Belfast or Larne. The railway company was quickly disabused of this idea by the Post Office.

In a minute of the 6th June 1868, the Treasury was forced to concede that the railway companies had performed their part of the 1856 agreement, but argued that there had been significant changes in the situation. The Treasury also accepted that "the harbour at Portpatrick, notwithstanding the expenditure of a very large sum of public money, has been reported by the Board of Trade to be in its present state dangerous and unsuitable for a night service; it has been found impossible to establish the service via Portpatrick and Donaghadee, as originally contemplated, so as to make it a safe and efficient service, without a further and heavy cost to the public in the extension and maintenance of Portpatrick Harbour, and the payment of a subsidy for the service quite out of proportion to the advantages now to be gained by it; and as the abandonment of the route will seriously affect the interest of the two railway companies, and have the effect of rendering worthless the expenditure incurred by the Portpatrick Railway Company in making the seven miles of railway between Stranraer and Portpatrick, My Lords are of the opinion that both railway companies have a just claim to compensation".

Compensation to the B&CDR had been agreed in July 1867. The Treasury agreed to make a loan of £166,666 to pay off the debentures of the company as they came due. The B&CDR had an annual interest rate of 5% and the government loan carried an interest rate of $3\frac{1}{2}\%$.

In November 1867, the PR rather disingenuously argued that the compensation to the PR should be based on a mileage comparison (22 miles for the B&CDR compared to 62 for the PR (Castle Douglas-Portpatrick). This would translate into a subsidised loan of some £470,000 instead of the proposed unconditional grant of £25,000.

Three months later, in February 1868, the Treasury replied, in essence suggesting that the PR "take the money and run" since there were no conditions attached and that it was surely more attractive than the uncertainties attaching to a mail contract. The Treasury also pointed out that the B&CDR had accepted the invitation to negotiate while the PR had not. In June 1868, the PR accepted the Treasury's next offer: an unconditional grant of £20,000 plus a low-interest loan of £153,000.

The Treasury observed that nothing in the agreement just reached prevented the PR from pressing ahead with operating the Portpatrick route and convincing the Post Master General of the advantages of sending mail through Portpatrick. Perhaps it was the turn of the Treasury to be disingenuous, but was this, in fact, about to happen?

5. A DREAM REALISED?

The dream of 1856 saw railways linking both Portpatrick and Donaghadee with major centres of commerce, industry and population. Steamships would provide an efficient service conveying passengers and mail over the short sea route.

A shadow of this dream began to form in the spring of 1867 when agitation started on the Irish side for establishing a steamship service. Mr. John Jamieson was an outspoken critic of the attempts to link Stranraer with Larne and Belfast and in May 1866 he had organised an excursion by the paddle steamer/tug *Terrible*. She crossed from Donaghadee and berthed in the new basin. Her passengers climbed up to the town station where a train waited to take them to visit Castle Kennedy. In March 1868, Jamieson demonstrated how short the short sea route was when with four companions he rowed from Donaghadee to Portpatrick on his way to the general meeting in Stranraer of the Portpatrick Railway.

In January 1868, the PR had been forced to abandon its second attempt at linking Stranraer with Northern Ireland (The first attempt with the paddler *Briton*, ceased on 31st December, 1863). The former blockade runners *Fannie* and *Alice* had been sailing between Stranraer and Belfast from December 1865 until the end of January

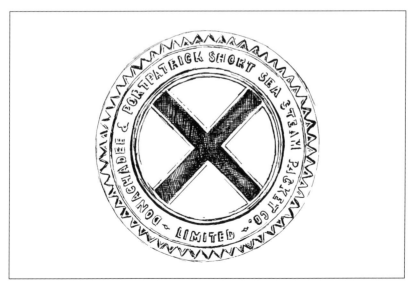

**Seal of the Donaghadee & Portpatrick Short Sea Steam
Packet Company, Limited.**

1868 by which time both paddlers were out of service with mechanical problems. Both were patched up sufficiently by June 1868 to sai from Stranraer to Bowling Harbour for layup while a buyer could be found. So, in July 1868, the board of the PR was prepared to consider a prospectus received from the Donaghadee & Portpatrick Short Sea Steam Packet Company, Ltd. The company had been organised in May by Murphy & Co of Queen's Square, Belfast, whose manager was Henry Gowans. Unlike many of today's companies, the name tells us what the promoters had in mind as they set about raising £10,000 of capital. The PR board met with a delegation from the packet company, including John Jamieson, and in return for the right to appoint two directors to the board, the railway company agreed to make a loan to the D&PSSSPC. The loan, interest-free for five years, was to be for the lesser of £5,000 or half the cost of the ship placed on the route.

There was some slick footwork since the D&PSSSPC purchased the steamer *Dolphin* on the 9th July 1868 from David Hutcheson & Co., of Glasgow. Built and engined in 1849 by Tod & McGregor, Partick, she had traded, as *Islay*, between Glasgow and the Western Isles of Scotland. Hutcheson had acquired her in February 1868 as a stop-gap and renamed her *Dolphin* to free up the name for a new steamer. Her employment in the first half of 1868 had been sporadic: Glasgow - Islay in April, and on charter in June to the Glasgow & Stranraer S P Co between the title ports. *Dolphin* was then laid up in Bowling Harbour.

Earlier it was noted that the new basin at Portpatrick was designed with steam packets of up to 150 feet in mind. So, at 172 feet, "length along keel," plus an elaborate bowsprit, *Dolphin* would be a tight fit within the basin. As it turned out, *Dolphin* was the most substantial vessel ever to use the harbour at Portpatrick.

Her purchase papers were signed on Thursday, 9th July, and *Dolphin*, with Captain George Dorman, made her first arrival at Portpatrick from Donaghadee on Saturday, 11th July, 1868. *Dolphin* arrived at Portpatrick in mid-afternoon after a crossing which occupied just less than two hours. The village put out the flags and provided a gun salute to welcome *Dolphin* and her excursionists and once *Dolphin* was berthed, "gentlemen met in her cabin and drank to the success of the venture". Was the dream at last to be realised?

On Monday, 13th July, a double daily service (excepting Sundays) started with departures from Donaghadee at 0900 and 1515, and from Portpatrick at 1225 and 1840. Train connections were advertised at both ends and an excursion fare of 5/- (25p) offered between Belfast and Portpatrick. The return fare for passengers with access to the cabin was 4/- (20p) and 2/- (10p) in steerage. A special train ran from

Portpatrick on arrival of the morning sailing. The train took excursionists to Stranraer and to Castle Kennedy station, just beyond Stranraer. Another attraction on offer was Dunskey House, the nearby home of Sir Edward Hunter Blair, which was "thrown open to visitors" on Mondays and Saturdays.

Stranraer Cattle Show fell at the end of *Dolphin's* first week and on Friday, 17th July, two hundred passengers crossed to Portpatrick where a train from the town station conveyed them to Stranraer. In August, an extra sailing from Portpatrick at 0700 on Thursdays provided a day excursion from the Scottish side with four hours in Belfast. The excursion was offered specially on Saturday, 15th August, when about two hundred passengers left Stranraer by special train shortly after 0600 hours.

The Caledonian Railway, which must have been questioning the wisdom of its investment in the PR, saw a possibility of salvaging something once the D&PSSSPC service started. The CR arranged for carriages to travel on the steep branch line linking the harbour station with the town station at Portpatrick. This arrangement appears to have been implemented in September 1868 and for two weeks from the 11th September the adverts promised that "the train now comes alongside the

DONAGHADEE AND PORTPATRICK
SHORT-SEA STEAM-PACKET CO. (LIMITED).

OPENING EXCURSION TRIP
OF THE
DONAGHADEE AND PORTPATRICK STEAM-
PACKET SERVICE
TO
STRANRAER AND CASTLE KENNEDY,
On SATURDAY, 11th Inst.

EXCURSIONISTS WILL BE CONVEYED BY the 10-45 a.m. Train from Belfast to Donaghadee; thence by the Company's splendid Paddle-steamer "DOLPHIN;" sailing from Donaghadee at Twelve o'clock Noon; and on arrival in Portpatrick, Passengers will be forwarded by Special Train to Stranraer and Castle Kennedy.
Train leave Stranraer and Castle Kennedy at 5-30 p.m. for Portpatrick, on arrival of which the Steamer will sail for Donaghadee, where a Special Train will be in waiting to convey Passengers to Belfast.
Fare from Belfast to Portpatrick and back, ... 5s.
Fare from Donaghadee to Portpatrick and back, ... 4s.
Fare from Portpatrick to Stranraer or Castle Kennedy and back, ... 1s.
Tickets—Belfast to Portpatrick only and back—limited to 300—to be had at the County Down Railway Station. Passengers by this Excursion travel First Class on County Down Railway,
Refreshments can be had on board the Steamer at moderate rates.
HENRY GOWAN, Agent,
29, Queen's Square.

DAYLIGHT AND SHORT-SEA PASSAGE.

TWO SERVICES EACH WAY DAILY
BETWEEN
DONAGHADEE AND PORTPATRICK.

TIME OCCUPIED LESS THAN TWO HOURS.

ON AND AFTER MONDAY, THE 13TH July, the Splendid Paddle Steamer "DOLPHIN" will Sail Twice each way DAILY.
From Donaghadee at 9·0 a.m. and 3·15 p.m., Irish time.
From Portpatrick at 12·25 and 6·40 p.m, Greenwich time.
Through Trains for all the principal Stations in England and Scotland leave Portpatrick at 1·10 and 6·15 p.m., and arrive there at 11·50 a.m. and 5·5 p.m.
County Down Railway Company's Trains in connection with the Steamer leave Belfast for Donaghadee at 7·45 a.m. and 1·40 p.m., and Donaghadee for Belfast at 4·25 and 8·50 p.m.
FARES BETWEEN DONAGHADEE AND PORTPATRICK:
Single—Cabin, ... 3s. Steerage, ... 1s 6d.
Return—Cabin, ... 4s. Steerage, ... 2s.
Passengers booked through between Portpatrick and the principal stations in England and Scotland.
A Special Train will run Daily with Excursionists from Portpatrick to Castle Kennedy on arrival of the morning Steamer.
For further particulars, apply to
HENRY GOWAN, Agent, Portpatrick, Donaghadee, and 29,
6668   Queen's Square, Belfast.

Advertisement for the steamer *Dolphin* from the Belfast Newsletter of 10 July 1868.

steamer at Portpatrick". As far as can be ascertained, this was the only time when passengers were actually conveyed by train on the harbour branch.

Around Monday, 7th September, the frequency of sailings dropped to one a day, leaving Donaghadee at 1100, though by the end of the month the time was 0900. The return fare was increased to 6/6 ($32^1/_2$p) in the cabin and 3/6 ($17^1/_2$p) in steerage. During the first week of September, *Dolphin* gave two excursions from Donaghadee to the Isle of Man. On Wednesday, 2nd September, Peel was the destination and on the Friday a two-day excursion was given to Douglas, with the return on Saturday. Excursionists wishing more time on the island could travel out on the Wednesday to Peel and return from Douglas on the Saturday.

Interestingly, there were no reports of interruptions on account of weather. But the summer was not free of incident. As *Dolphin* entered Donaghadee Harbour on the evening of Friday, 25th September, 1868, she took the ground in the vicinity of the old quay and remained there until the next morning. The first appearance of no damage to the ship turned out to be incorrect and a drydock inspection in Belfast led to repairs lasting well into October. *Dolphin's* next crossing to Portpatrick was on Saturday, 31st October. Monday's Belfast Newsletter carried the headline "Melancholy Occurrence at Donaghadee". As *Dolphin* entered Donaghadee Harbour on the Saturday evening, her bowsprit came in contact with the crane on the quay. The bowsprit splintered and killed a young lad who happened to be standing near the crane. Witnesses said the engineer was slow in reversing the engines, but the newspaper opined that the "fault is distributed over other parties" and both the captain and engineer were briefly held in jail.

It is not clear whether *Dolphin* sailed again for D&PSSSPC but a photograph shows her, minus bowsprit, at Portpatrick. If she did sail after the fatal accident, it was for a very short period.

In late September, the D&PSSSPC reported that four thousand passengers had travelled by *Dolphin*. But, there was no mail and no indication that the passenger traffic was other than local and excursion. With reliable and frequent sailings between Belfast and Ardrossan, Greenock, and Glasgow there was little chance of a viable all-year-round service on the short sea route. *Dolphin* was laid up in Belfast and her next sailing was from Belfast in mid-September 1869 when Husum on the North Sea coast of Germany was the destination. The D&PSSSPC had sold *Dolphin* for the disappointingly low price of £1,700 to a London merchant who employed her between London and Baltic ports.

The summer of 1869 had seen little activity on the Portpatrick route. The paddler *Earl of Arran* began her Belfast-Bangor sailings on

The D&PSSSPCo's *Dolphin* berthed in the new basin at Portpatrick in 1868. In the foreground the lines of the harbour branch are visible; also the culvert accommodating the Dinvin Burn. In the distance the South Pier can be seen, complete with two lighthouses.

Saturday, 15th May, and spent the previous two days giving day excursions from Donaghadee to Portpatrick, leaving Donaghadee at 0845 on arrival of the 0730 train from Belfast. The excursionists could travel by

```
┌─────────────────────────────────────────┐
│              SHIPPING.                    │
│ ───────────────────────────────────────  │
│          SHORT-SEA PASSAGE.               │
│  STRANRAER AND RHINS OF GALLOWAY          │
│        AGRICULTURAL SHOW.                 │
│  THE FAST STEAMER "RELIANCE,"             │
│     Captain WALLS, will Sail from Donaghadee│
│  on arrival of 7-30 a m. Train from Belfast, on│
│  FRIDAY, 22nd July, 1870, for above Show. │
│     Sea Passage, 90 minutes.              │
│     Will Return from Show in time for last train to│
│  Belfast.                                 │
│  ─────────────────────────────────────   │
│    Fares (Return Tickets)—Cabin, 3s; Steerage, 2s.│
│    Donaghadee, July 19, 1870.       7167  │
└─────────────────────────────────────────┘
```

**Advertisement for the steamer *Reliance* from the
Belfast Newsletter of 20th July, 1870.**

the 1010 train from Portpatrick to visit the grounds of Castle Kennedy, near Stranraer.

In October 1869, the D&PSSSPC reported a loss of £2,552 during its short life but, undaunted, approached the PR and B&CDR with a view to combining in the purchase of a steamer and re-opening the route in the spring of 1870. Nothing came of this and the D&PSSSPC joined the pile of ventures seduced by the fatal allure of the short sea route. The same fate befell the attempt by the promoters of Portpatrick and North of Ireland Steam Packet Company to interest the PR early in 1870 in investing in the company.

But *Dolphin* had shown that the route might have some potential as a summer excursion route and the owners of the small steamer *Reliance* placed her on a daily round trip in mid-July 1870. *Reliance* left Donaghadee around 0900 each day after the arrival of a train from Belfast. The return sailing from Portpatrick was at 1700. *Reliance* was a member of that once-common class of steamer which did double duty as a tug and a passenger steamer. She was considerably smaller than *Dolphin*, 101 feet in length compared to 172 feet, and the Galloway Advertiser guardedly remarked, "though a small steamer [*Reliance*] seems well adapted to passenger trade during the summer". *Reliance* was commanded by Captain John Walls.

On Saturday, 13th August, 1870, *Reliance* reversed her route and left Portpatrick at 0800, connecting with a train at 0730 from Stranraer. At Donaghadee a train connected for Belfast. The return sailing from Donaghadee was scheduled for 1900. Special fares were offered on the B&CDR: return tickets at single fares, but the advert baldly stated "usual fares will be charged on Portpatrick Railway". The last sailing by *Reliance* was on Saturday, 3rd September, 1870.

A group identified as "promoters of Portpatrick and Donaghadee" arranged for the small Belfast Lough steamer, *Shamrock*, another tug/passenger steamer, to make two round trips from Portpatrick to Donaghadee on Saturday, 13th May, 1871. The first departure from Portpatrick was at 0700 and four hours later she was back for her second trip. On Wednesday, 24th May, the Queen's Birthday Holiday, *Shamrock* gave a day trip from Portpatrick to Peel, Isle of Man. *Shamrock* returned to Portpatrick to repeat her 13th May schedule on the 22nd and 23rd June.

It was mid-August before a "regular" service was attempted. *Aber*, a steamer similar to *Reliance*, also owned by W. Nicholson & Sons, and under the command of Captain John Walls began a daily service. But her time on the short sea route was brief. There was a lot of mist near the Irish coast on Tuesday, 29th August, 1871, and the liner *Prussian* of the Allan Line ran into *Aber*, almost slicing her in two amidships. *Aber* sank within minutes. Her seventeen passengers and eight crew were safely landed at Donaghadee. Thus ended dramatically yet another attempt to exploit the short sea route.

Developments at Stranraer now removed any incentive to continue attempting to maintain a link between Portpatrick and Donaghadee. By the spring of 1871, the PR and the Belfast & Northern Counties Railway had negotiated the re-opening of the route between Stranraer and Larne. The PR was to put into the venture half the compensation received from the government following the abandonment of the Portpatrick route. On the 1st July, 1872, the Larne & Stranraer Steamboat Company Ltd placed the new paddle steamer *Princess Louise* on a daily (except Sunday) round trip between the title ports. Train connections were given at each end. The Stranraer-Larne link was to continue without break until 1995 when Belfast became the Irish terminus.

The provision of a reliable daily service from Stranraer with a comfortable steamer of more than 200 feet in length and a reasonable speed (though the *Louise* could eat her way through a lot of coal) met the needs of most local traffic and even a tug/passenger steamer between tows could not make an honest summer penny at Portpatrick.

This proved to be the case when an attempt was made in 1873 to operate the Portpatrick route. Andrews & Co. of Belfast were behind this attempt. In December 1865, representatives of the firm had approached the PR with a proposal of co-operation with the railway company on the crossing. But the PR was firmly under the financial thumb of the

Caledonian Railway and obliged to do its bidding. The CR had made a significant investment in the PR in 1864 and in 1865 had purchased the two paddlers *Fannie* and *Alice*, recently returned from successful careers as blockade runners during the American Civil War. The CR had instructed the PR to place these paddle steamers on a daily service between Stranraer and Belfast. In December 1865, when Andrews & Co. approached the PR, *Fannie* had just started on the route and her sister was expected soon. The CR left no doubt in the mind of the PR that the Belfast route had to be a success. The PR's protests to the CR that the Portpatrick crossing had also to be maintained fell on deaf CR ears and the overtures from Andrews & Co. in 1865 had been rejected.

Despite the major changes since 1865, Andrews & Co. placed their paddle steamer *Avalon* on the short sea route in June 1873. *Avalon* made her first departure from Donaghadee at 0900 on Tuesday, 10th June, 1873, after the arrival of the train from Belfast. The return time from Portpatrick was 1730. The advertised crossing time of $1^1/_2$ hours proved optimistic. The service ceased on Saturday, 12th July, after just over five weeks. The reason given in the press was the refusal on the part of the railway companies to provide "necessary facilities". Presumably this referred to excursion fares and it is likely that the PR was the main culprit since the B&CDR had nothing to lose. We have to assume that *Avalon* was yet another tug-boat trying to earn some marginal revenue but she has eluded identification (One writer has identified her as a paddle steamer of that name built in 1865 for the Great Eastern Railway Company for its North Sea routes out of Harwich. But the Great Eastern vessel's length of 240 feet makes this extremely unlikely).

Shortly after *Avalon* gave up, the railway link to the harbour at Portpatrick disappeared. In September 1874, the PR board agreed to lift the rails of the branch and transfer them to Newton Stewart. In May 1889, the board agreed that a piece of "waste land" at Portpatrick could be rented out for use as a bowling green. This waste land was the site of the harbour branch terminus. So, today we find tennis courts and a bowling green under the cliff face where there should have been the raison d'être of the PR. Very few remains of the harbour branch can be identified. One is the embankment just above where Main Street becomes Holm Street and where the line crossed on an iron bridge. The bridge was removed in 1902. At the north-west corner of the harbour, the culvert containing the Dinvin Burn has become increasingly exposed and eroded. Now, a curious archway which used to be the seaward end of the culvert survives to show the boundary of the harbour railway area.

To report on the last attempt to maintain the short sea route we must "fast forward" to 1891 when a paddle steamer with the unpromis-

Terrible in the inner basin is photographed from McCook's Craig.

ing name of *Terrible* appeared at Donaghadee. Whether this is the same *Terrible* that Mr. John Jamieson used on an isolated excursion in 1866 is open to question though the 1891 *Terrible* does appear to have been yet one more of that breed of paddler combining towing duties with those of a passenger carrier. She had been operating in the upper firth of the Clyde for several years and is reported, in 1884, as having a passenger certificate for 540.

James McGladdery of Portpatrick is identified as the promoter behind the scheme to have *Terrible* provide a daily service between Donaghadee and Portpatrick for the months of July, August and September in 1891. *Terrible* did not get off to a good start. She left Bowling Harbour on the Clyde on the 27th June for a service advertised to start that day and she managed as far as Cairnryan before being brought to a stop by mechanical problems. *Terrible* eventually reached Portpatrick on Wednesday, 1st July.

Terrible's initial timetable had an 0900 departure from Donaghadee, with morning and evening train connections from and to Belfast. The cabin return fare was 4/- (20p) and 2/6 (12 $^1/_2$p) in steerage. But by the 12th July, the service was advertised as leaving the Irish side at 1030 on weekdays and 1115 on Sundays with return times from Scotland at 1800 and 1630 respectively.

Wednesday, 15th July, 1891, was a holiday in Newtownards and several took advantage of the revived opportunity of sailing across to Portpatrick. The Newtownards Chronicle reported that the crossing was made in a couple of hours and "as the day was brilliantly fine and the sea smooth, nothing but good fellowship prevailed on board". At Portpatrick many went by train to Stranraer. The Chronicle concluded that "if the merits of this trip were better known we could with confidence predict a good season for the promoter, Mr. McGladdery".

But all was not well and *Terrible* lived up to her name. Repeated mechanical trouble caused the ship to miss trips and the service was abandoned in late July. An acrimonious legal dispute broke out between Mr. McGladdery and the owners of *Terrible*, Thomas Clavering & Co of Glasgow, with the pursuer successfully claiming that his losses were attributable to the unsuitable nature of the steamer for the route.

Thus ended yet another and, so far, the final attempt at a regular service exploiting the short sea route.

6. A QUIET CENTURY

While the nineteenth century at Portpatrick had been one characterised by optimism, dashed hopes, frenetic activity punctuated by periods of idleness, and profligacy with public money, the twentieth century was one of acceptance that the most Portpatrick and Donaghadee could aspire to was the role of quiet family holiday resorts. There were occasional spurts of activity causing nostalgic reflections on the old days. The activity was usually in the context of strike breaking.

In the unsettled days following the First World War, industrial strife caused much upheaval around the country. In 1921, a coalminers' strike dragged on for weeks and the Ministry of Transport, in order to conserve coal and also possibly to cause inconvenience and so reduce public support for the miners' cause, closed down several shipping routes. The Stranraer-Larne service was withdrawn between the 16th April and the 9th July 1921 — causing greater disruption than had ever occurred during the war. The overnight services from Glasgow and Ardrossan to Belfast were also cancelled, leaving no connection between Scotland and Ireland.

"An enterprising Belfast gentleman", Mr. William Seabrooke, saw an opportunity of resurrecting the short sea route and placed three motor boats on the crossing (One wonders if these anonymous boats were normally plying between Donaghadee and the Copeland Islands. The islands were not evacuated until the late 1950s). The boats lacked passenger certificates for the route and so were limited to twelve passengers. The service started around Friday, 23rd May, and consisted of an 0900 departure from Donaghadee after the arrival of the 0730 train from Belfast. Three hours were allowed for the trip. The return from Portpatrick was scheduled for 1500 and connected at Donaghadee with a train reaching Belfast at 2035. The press reported that Mr. Seabrooke planned to charter a small steamer should circumstances warrant the step. There is no indication that such a step was taken and the motor boat service, we assume, was discontinued once the Stranraer *Princess Victoria* returned to service on Saturday, 9th July, 1921.

Isolation can have its advantages. In the summer months both before and after the Second World War, it was not unusual for Portpatrick fishermen to take a break by offering excursions along the coast and even to Donaghadee (The matter of passenger certificates probably did not receive much attention). Also, the lack of Sunday sailings between Stranraer and Larne provided an opportunity for the Portpatrick fishermen to carry newspapers over to Donaghadee — the Scots enjoying the fleshpots of County Down still needed their weekly encounter with Oor Wullie. It was the regularity of the newspaper runs that got the attention of the "authorities" and it was deemed that the enterprising fishermen had gone too far when, in June 1952, they planned their annual trip for local motor cycle enthusiasts to the Isle of Man for the TT races. The Board of Trade stepped in and the trips were cancelled when the fishermen could produce neither passenger certificates for their boats nor lifesaving equipment. This attention would cause the fishermen to stick to their authorised trade — at least for a time.

It was a seamen's strike in July 1960 that brought activity back to the Portpatrick route. As in 1921, open motor boats from Donaghadee and Bangor ran across the channel and carried mainly holidaymakers stranded by the strike. The national press carried photographs of rain-soaked travellers with luggage, lurching down the steps in Abernethy's basin towards a boat with, mercifully, a canvas covering. Another photograph showed one of the motor boats leaving Portpatrick harbour and flying a large Northern Ireland flag at the bow. One newspaper reported, "During Saturday, 16th July, about a hundred people sailed in from Donaghadee and an equal number left Portpatrick for the return. The only apparent distress to their ranks had been wrought by the boisterous swell of the North Channel. Handkerchiefs waved and greetings carried across the water until the boats rode the first swell of the open sea. As though by order, coat collars turned up and the boats sailed on in silence for the 21-mile crossing".

During the protracted seamen's strike in the summer of 1966, the chartered Swedish passenger and car ferry, Stena Nordica, continued to operate between Stranraer and Larne for the Caledonian Steam Packet Company (Irish Services) Ltd. Even so, fishing vessels did carry much freight between Portpatrick and Donaghadee.

Lorry drivers in Northern Ireland went on strike in November 1974 and fishing boats found it was more lucrative to carry merchandise than to go fishing. The local press reported that on Tuesday, 12th November, five fishing boats were ferrying millions of cigarettes from Ulster. By mid-day, twelve boats had been observed at Portpatrick unloading clothing from Marks & Spencer and loading machine parts and oil for the return trip.

The lorries trundled down Portpatrick's Main Street again for a couple of weeks in May 1988 when a seamen's strike tied up the Stranraer and Cairnryan fleets. As in 1974, the primary concern was movement of freight since passengers now had air travel as an option.

A less savoury traffic was stopped in January 1976 when the Special Branch seized a 30-foot cabin cruiser at Portpatrick which was claimed to be involved in gun running to Ireland. On a more frivolous note, a place in the Guinness Book of Records was earned by TV personality Peter Duncan and Steve Good when they "drove" a converted Volkswagen from Portpatrick to Donaghadee on Sunday, 10th March, 1985. The "craft" made part of the journey under tow, having capsized in the force five winds. But, we are assured, the VW beetle was righted for the final few yards (The press report did not reveal which category Messrs. Duncan and Good qualified for!).

There have been several "close calls" during the century. In 1970, the Coastal Cruising Association chartered the turbine steamer *King George V* from David MacBrayne Ltd. for a day excursion from Bangor to Donaghadee and Portpatrick. But in the event, it was deemed impossible to call at either end of the short sea route and the cruise operated on Saturday, 16th May, from Bangor was towards Portpatrick and then back by Donaghadee and the Copelands Channel.

Even though *King George V* could not call at Donaghadee, the port did receive occasional calls from excursion steamers before and after the May 1970 attempt. These vessels either came from or went to Larne, Belfast and the Isle of Man. The scale of the harbour and the increasing presence of small private pleasure craft in the harbour required that the vessels tied up across the entrance. In recent years, Donaghadee has been a calling place for the preserved excursion ships, the motor vessel *Balmoral* and the paddle steamer *Waverley*. On several occasions, *Waverley* has taken excursions to the mouth of the harbour at Portpatrick but has never called. *Waverley's* first excursion to "off" Portpatrick was from Ayr and Cairnryan on Sunday, 15th May, 1977.

(On a personal note. The first time I saw Portpatrick from the sea was in May 1977 when I was purser on the *Waverley*. We were returning from a week working out of Liverpool and heading for Ayr. At about ten o'clock at night we passed close to the harbour entrance and for a minute saw the bright lights of Portpatrick between the cliffs. The "eye of the needle" aspect of the harbour entrance is striking when seen from the sea.)

In 1971, an unsuccessful attempt was made to interest the privately-owned Scottish ferry operator, Western Ferries, in opening a service for passengers and vehicles between Portpatrick and Bangor.

Plans were announced in November 1976 for a £15 million scheme to link Portpatrick and Donaghadee. The plan was to employ an SRN 4 Mountbatten class hovercraft capable of carrying nearly 300 passengers and 38 cars. Behind this scheme was Ulster bus operator Neil Oliver who had been instrumental in introducing direct bus links between Belfast and London. A nineteenth century battle was resurrected when residents of the village of Portlogan petitioned to be the Scottish end of the route. Some local authority officials were of the opinion that Cairnryan would be even better. In the event, the plans were not pursued.

During the first half of the twentieth century, Donaghadee, unlike Portpatrick, continued to be a port of call for several coastal cargo boats, usually carrying coal. The closing in April 1950 of the railway to Donaghadee and the branch down to the harbour, made Donaghadee much less attractive for the coal traffic, and calls became very infrequent.

The sea continued its relentless destruction of Portpatrick Harbour. During a storm early in January 1991, a stump, the sole remaining trace of Vetch's patch-up of Smeaton's pier of the 1770s, finally collapsed. Later in the same year, the perennial problem of the breakwater joining McCook's Craig to the north pier required attention and a causeway was built and another attempt also made to arrest the beach erosion on the west side of the basin.

The more things change, the more they stay the same!

BIBLIOGRAPHY

Cunningham, R.R.: *Portpatrick Through the Ages* (Stranraer, 1997)

Green, E.R.R.: *The Industrial Archaeology of County Down* (HMSO, Belfast, 1963)

Haldane, A.R.B.: *Three Centuries of Scottish Posts* (Edinburgh University Press, Edinburgh, 1971)

MacHaffie, F.G.: *The Short Sea Route* (T. Stephenson & Sons Ltd., Prescot, 1975)

Rennie, J.: *The Theory, Formation and Construction of British and Foreign Harbours*, 2 volumes (John Weale, London, 1854)

Reports of the late John Smeaton, F.R.S. 3 volumes (Longman, Hurst, Rees, Orme, and Brown, London, 1812)

Smith, D. L.: *The Little Railways of South-West Scotland* (David & Charles (Publishers) Ltd., Newton Abbott, 1969)

Stevenson, J.: *Two Centuries of Life in Down 1600-1800* (McCaw, Stevenson & Orr, Ltd., Belfast and Dublin, 1920)

Thorne, H.D.: *Rails to Portpatrick* (T. Stephenson & Sons Ltd., Prescot, 1976)

Government records, papers, etc.

Parliamentary Papers:

 1820 (252), IX *Report on the Harbours at Donaghadee and Portpatrick*

 1821 (556), XVI *Donaghadee and Portpatrick Harbours*

 1830 (647), XIV *Twenty-second Report of the Commissioners of Revenue Inquiry*

 1831-32 (716), XVII *Report of the Select Committee on Post Communication with Ireland*

 1860 (123), LXII *Portpatrick & Donaghadee Harbours*, &c.

 1867-68 (356), LXIII *Portpatrick and Donaghadee Harbours*

Portpatrick Harbour - Copy Letter Book, Alexander Hannay to James Abernethy, 1863-1865 (Stranraer Museum)

Portpatrick Packet Station - Copy Letter Book, 1844-47 (Stranraer Museum)

The Register of the Privy Council of Scotland, Series I, 1545-1624; Series II, 1625-1660; Series III, 1661-1691

ACKNOWLEDGMENTS

When writing The Short Sea Route in the 1970s, I benefited immensely from correspondence with the late James McEwan of Bearsden, who placed at my disposal his broad knowledge of the transport history of south-west Scotland. In preparing this publication, I have been fortunate to have access to Mr. Ross Cunningham of Portpatrick who has also given generously of his time and knowledge. He has also kindly agreed to the reproduction of some of the Portpatrick maps appearing in his Portpatrick Through the Ages.

Various individuals have kindly given permission to reproduce photographs. Mr. Tom Ross of Bangor has kindly consented to the reproduction of the 1799 passport issued to Mr. Arthur Hill Coates and the seal of the Donaghadee & Portpatrick Short Sea Steam Packet Co., Ltd., both of which are in his possession.

I gratefully acknowledge assistance received from the Faculty Development Committee (Dr. Greg. Delemeester, chair) of Marietta College, Ohio, to cover research expenses.

Finally, I acknowledge that working in the United States of America for a quarter of a century has left me with a mixed vocabulary and style. I have tried to avoid "Americanisms", but if you find a "harbor" where you expect a "harbour", etc. I apologize/apologise.

THIS BOOK has been published by the Stranraer and District Local History Trust which was constituted in 1998 at the instigation of Stranraer and District Chamber of Commerce.

The Trust would like to thank Mr Alan McFarlane, Stranraer, for work undertaken for this publication.

Previous Trust publications:

Stranraer in World War Two
— Archie Bell.

The Loss of the Princess Victoria
— Jack Hunter.

The Cairnryan Military Railway 1941-1959
— Bill Gill.

A Peep at Stranraer's Past
—Donnie Nelson.

Royal Burgh of Stranraer -1617-1967-2000
— John S. Boyd, Jack Hunter, Donnie Nelson, Christine L. Wilson.

Don't Plague The Ferryman.
— Trevour Boult

Trust Membership Fee for 2001-2002 is £4.

This entitles members to a discount of 20% on one copy of each publication when purchased from the Secretary.

Applications for membership, with subscriptions, should be made to the Secretary, Mrs Christine Wilson, Tall Trees, London Road, Stranraer DG9 8BZ.

Telephone: (01776) 703101.

Membership 2001 - 2002

Mrs Sheelagh Afia
Miss S.I. Baldwin
Mrs Elaine Barton
Mr Archie Bell
Mrs Dorothy Bell
Mr Douglas Brown
Mr David B. Cairns
Mrs Emily Carruth
Mr John Carruth
Mr William Clelland
Mr Charles Collins
Mrs Harriet Collins
Mr J.P. Davis
Mr Bill Dougan
Mr Jim Ferguson
Miss Dora Gorman
Mrs Irene Grant
Mr Tom Hargreaves
Mr Richard Holme
Mr Peter Holmes
Mrs J. Hornsby-Bartlett
Mr Jack Hunter
Mr Ronnie Logan
Mr Andrew McCubbin

Mr Colin McCubbin
Mrs Nancy McLucas
Prof. John McQueen, Vice-Chairman
Mrs Margaret Matthews
Mr K. R. Muir
Mrs Lynn Nield
Mr Donnie Nelson, Chairman
Mrs Mae Nelson
Mr Alastair Penman
Mr John Pickin
Mrs Margaret Pratt
Mrs Helen Scott
Mr Tom A. Sexton
Mr J.D.Sharp
Mr P.N. Skinner
Mrs Renee Smith
Mr Bill Stanley
Mrs Sheila Stevenson
Mr Tom Stevenson, Hon. Treasurer
Mr David Williamson
Mrs ChristineWilson, Hon. Secretary
Mrs Elizabeth Wilson
Mr Eric Wilson
Mr William I. Wilson

Stranraer Chamber of Commerce